# THE VERY BEST OF BRITISH

# THE
# VERY BEST
## OF
# BRITISH

## NICHOLAS COURTNEY
*with drawings by John Ireland*

COLLINS
8 Grafton Street, London W1
1985

William Collins Sons & Co. Ltd
London * Glasgow * Sydney * Auckland
Toronto * Johannesburg

BRITISH LIBRARY CATALOGUING IN PUBLICATION DATA

Courtney, Nicholas
The very best of British.
1. Upper classes – Great Britain    2. Great
Britain – Social life and customs – 1945–
I. Title
941.085'.8'0880621          HT653.G7

First published 1985
© Nicholas Courtney 1985

ISBN 0-00-217337-9

Photoset in Linotron Palatino by
Rowland Phototypesetting Ltd
Bury St Edmunds, Suffolk
Made and printed in Great Britain by
William Collins Sons & Co. Ltd, Glasgow

# CONTENTS

# INTRODUCTION

It is a warm evening in late June; the full-length sash windows are open on to the terrace of the Palladian front, eighteenth-century addition to the Tudor mansion. The smell of newly-mown grass (the lawns are contemporary with the original house), vies with the sweet, cloying scent of climbing roses. The cooing of ring doves from the spinney below is audible above the snatches of conversation on the terrace – here cultured voices knowledgeably discussing art, there a rich Texan drawl. Standing beside an eighteenth-century stone urn (bursting with pink and white peonies), the young Earl, wearing the lightest of cashmere dinner jackets, welcomes the last of his guests, the beautiful Marquesa on the arm of a cleric. The old butler, black-jacketed with knife-edged, striped trousers, makes his way silently along the terrace and whispers into the young Countess's ear. Scooping up her glass of Dom Perignon '66, she leads her guests through the French windows into the dining room. Tonight, they dine off the gold plate.

This is not the opening of a Mills and Boon romantic novella, but a weekend scene, typical of anywhere in Britain today. On closer examination, the scene is even more typical. The house is about to go – a series of bad investments (mostly in the racier gaming houses) has forced the sale. It has already been sold as a time-sharing retreat for a very rich but minor sect from the Bible belt of the mid-West – the young Earl, who now works for one of the more unscrupulous of the great estate agents, conducted the deal himself. His dinner jacket, last worn by Ryan O'Neil, was left behind by the wardrobe department of the feature film company that rented the house for the tenth remake of *The Four Feathers*. The cultured voices discussing art come from representatives of the fine art auctioneers, who are about to dispose of the contents of the house. The beautiful Marquesa, who has her own catering company, has won the contract for the lunch marquee for the three-day sale. As for the butler, he is Filipino and the reason he whispers in the young Countess's ear is that she is the only one to understand pidgin English, having spent some time singing in the Far East. The Texan drawl is there to collect the gold plate that he is about to donate to the Metropolitan Museum (the gift is tax deductible). Being neither British nor a classicist, he would not understand the motto which, loosely translated, reads 'Whatever the foe, we will remain forever'. Despite minor setbacks, the young Earl will always live up to his motto, as his family has done for centuries.

Towards the end of the nineteenth century, the British Empire was at its height. Great Britain had bagged a quarter of the globe; she stood for all that was great and powerful, glorious and excellent. At home, her people lived secure in the knowledge that their lives were morally and socially correct – so long as any departure from the norm was not 'in front of the servants and did not frighten the horses'. Since that zenith, the Empire has gone, the country has become a minor power, British manufactured goods are no longer best and British sportsmen are rarely champions. What has remained, however, is stability, a healthy social system and, for the privileged few at the top, a traditional and amusing way of life.

To be a member of that *beau monde* does not depend solely on lineage, glamour, wealth or power, though something of this is necessary. It is a state of mind. The life, attitudes and social scene of the elite is an extension of the nursery; the bars of the Edwardian play-pen have gradually expanded to embrace the whole of an ordered and well-tried existence. All emotions, tastes, and enthusiasms have their roots in nursery days.

For example, children familiar with the dressing-up box and charades progress to tails at Eton or gowns at Winchester, don ceremonial regalia, mess kit in the Services, a morning coat for Ascot, a red coat to hunt, faded pastel colours for Henley, to the manner born. To those brought up on nursery food, it remains for ever preferred fare, which is why the smarter London clubs and City dining rooms continue to serve rice puddings, dumplings and sausages and mash. The horse plays an important part in nursery life – there is a theory that the British ride so well because as children they all had large rocking horses and spent much time acquiring a strong seat for later life. *Equus* looms large through adolescence and into later life.

It is confidence that sets apart the members of that upper echelon. It is in part at school or university but still more in the nursery that they have learned the 'rules' to live by, unwritten rules but nonetheless as clearly defined as if enshrined in the Bill of Rights or Magna Carta. They may not know right from wrong, but they know how to behave. However brash and ill-mannered they may be, they can turn on the charm when the need arises. Secure upon a pedestal of privilege – if a public school boy transgresses it is still a rag, if a comprehensive school boy does the same it is hooliganism – they condescend to the rest of humanity in the snug certainty that they possess quality denied to the lesser breeds without the law.

Money and power may largely have departed, but style remains; style teetering on the edge of vulgarity yet rarely tumbling over. The dictionary definition of 'style' reads: 'general characteristics and manner of an individual, group or period in practising any art, skill or sport; elegance of manner; correct mode of fashion'. Life as practised by the British upper classes is indeed elegant and correct – to some it may also appear vapid, artificial and socially irresponsible, but that, the British upper classes will explain, is a misapprehension based on jealousy. How could it not be, since the life led by the British upper classes is the Very Best of British?

# CHAPTER 1

# LONDON LIFE

London is the capital of Great Britain, as once it was the capital of the world – or so the British believed. It is in every way a capital city, the seat of power, the residence of the Sovereign, the centre of finance. Learning and the Arts, with a capital A, flourish in London; Oxford and Cambridge are planets twinkling in its system. London still attracts the cream of British society, as it has done since the first Roman invasion back in 55 BC, and provides a slightly seedy version of nineteenth-century society with pomp and circumstance, with political soirées and balls, clubs and private boxes, royal occasions and private revelry. London is for the rich and discerning.

That said, it is therefore rather odd that the British have always preferred the country – the country being everywhere that is over fifty miles from Charing Cross (in certain directions), and does not have a population of more than a few hundred. Unlike the French aristocracy, who found it intolerable to be dragged away from Versailles, the British nobility and gentry have always been addicted to life on their estates, often to the exclusion of all else. Even today, their attitude is not dissimilar to that nineteenth-century statesman, the eighth Duke of Devonshire, who, despite his political achievements, still averred that his proudest moment was when his prize sow won first prize at the County Show.

London is somewhere you go to from the country. It is nevertheless the centre of national life, the heartland of the Very Best of British. Whatever the reason for leaving the country to be in London – to sit in Parliament, a stay at Sister Agnes's [King

Edward VII's Hospital], to shop, to visit a tailor or even, God forbid, to work – life revolves around food and equally important, drink. All London social life, especially where conversation is expected and enjoyed, takes place either during, just before or just after a meal – anything else is merely an interlude between 'breakfast, dinner, lunch and tea'. The Very Best of British days in London could run thus:

## BREAKFAST

'Only dull people are brilliant at breakfast,' said Oscar Wilde, to whom he might have added high-powered politicians or business 'persons' had he been writing of today. In less exalted circles a solitary breakfast with a newspaper is infinitely preferable who-ever is on offer (there is, after all, the rest of the day and most of the night in which to be sociable).

There are few places in London where you can breakfast better than in your own home. Only there can you have what you really want, when you want it, unrestricted by licensing laws – if you go to an hotel, you cannot have Bucks' Fizz (champagne and fresh orange juice) until 10.30 and by that time, breakfast is 'off'. Only at home can you command silence, or listen to the crunch of your own cornflakes and the rustle of your own newspaper. Only at home can you guarantee the exact blend of your Formosa Oolong or Earl Grey tea, the strength of your medium roast Colombian Arabaca coffee, and, like that great Englishman, Phileas Fogg, the temperature of your toast (he liked his at 183°F). You will also have had the delight of choosing your marmalades from Fortnum and Mason's – their Sir Nigel's Vintage Orange Marmalade is highly recommended. So much for the light London breakfast. The 'great British breakfast', as traditional and lasting as the Monarchy and nearly as hard to find in the flesh, with its over-loaded sideboards of kidneys, kedgeree, three different egg dishes, bacon, sausages and mushrooms, belongs to the country, where intense activity and fresh air can work it off before lunch.

However good the food at the London hotels and clubs, break-fast is invariably disappointing. The Connaught is thought to be the best but, as you cannot book, you have to take pot luck on being given a table. Not strictly British, but nonetheless a London

institution, is the *Brasserie* in the Fulham Road, South Kensington, where *croissants* and strong coffee are served from 8 o'clock onwards. More important, as in all good French cafés, they have the newspapers mounted on sticks.

One of the principal joys of breakfast is the morning papers. Sadly the 'Royal Edition' of *The Times*, a hundred specially printed copies on whiter-than-white rag paper for the likes of the Queen, the Prime Minister and the Archbishop of Canterbury, was discontinued at the end of 1969. No impassioned entreaties to Rupert Murdoch, the patron; Charles Douglas-Home, the editor; or, more important, the head of the chapel of SOGAT '82, will have the practice revived, even for you. You will have to make do with having your copy ironed – to fix the newsprint rather than for any sensual pleasure you may derive from a crisply ironed sheet.

The crossword complete, you have a few hours to fill in before you repair for lunch. There are many options open to you, not least a little sartorial shopping.

## CLOTHES

Beau Brummell, that arbiter of taste, believed that the best dressed men were the ones whose clothes were so immaculate that you did not notice them. The Brummell rule still applies today: it is one of the ironies of life that those who are noticed sartorially are those who are incorrectly dressed.

The top London tailors have enjoyed a world-wide reputation for centuries. Everything from the micro-chip to the flying-boat has been copied and improved upon by the Japanese, yet they are still many widths away when it comes to reproducing an English bespoke tailored suit. That is why the area bounded by Regent Street and Bond Street that includes Cork Street, Old Burlington Street and Savile Row itself, is known as the Golden Mile of London and is full of smiling Japanese, dapper Italians and traditionally-minded Americans as well as the more discerning (and richer) British.

To join the ranks of the well dressed, a stroll along Savile Row is all that is needed. If you go to number 15, the premises of Henry Poole, you will find one of the most eminent tailors in the street, and therefore in the world. To have a suit built [made] there is a relaxed and rewarding experience. The place has the atmosphere of a gentleman's club, a hangover from the days of the original Henry Poole, known to his customers as 'Old Pooley', whose patrons flocked to his shop 'between 3.30 and 5.00 p.m. to partake of his fine claret and hock and to puff "Pooley's cigars".' When Disraeli immortalised Mr Poole in his novel, *Endymion* as Mr Vigo, 'the most fashionable tailor in London . . . consummate in his art . . . neither pretentious nor servile, . . . with becoming respect for others and himself', he could easily have been describing Angus Cundey, the present owner and descendant of Poole. Although you will not be given a cigar or a glass of chilled hock, you will certainly be treated to the best service.

When you make up your mind what kind of suit you want, you will be shown samples of the finest cloth; the top worsteds, expensive cashmeres, or their own special tweed that comes from a secret Scottish mill. You then discuss the style of your suit with your assistant and the cutter, who has emerged from where he is working at the back of the shop. Once you are assigned to a cutter, like your black labrador, he is faithful for life. Fortunately, cutters live for a very long time. He will measure you in a way that will pick up even the slightest irregularities in your shape, conducting a muttered dialogue with his acolyte as he works: '42', '42', '34', '34'; 'VRB', 'VRB'. Only under cross-examination will he admit apologetically that 'VRB' stands for Very Round Back – 'Of course not what *you* mean by a round back, sir. Just a tailor's term.' You can have anything you want, a large inside pocket if you have a large wallet, a special pocket for your hunter [watch]. You will then choose your silk lining, nothing too garish for a dark suit. A feature of a bespoke tailored suit is the buffalo horn buttons.

In about two weeks, a card will come to say that your suit is ready for the first fitting. By now you have established a certain rapport with your cutter; it is not unknown for his clients to tell secrets to him in the same way as women confess to their hairdressers. If you are a first time client, it may be necessary to return for a second fitting, but usually the cutter has done a good job and can have the suit finished. The operation is quite quick, taking between five and six weeks. For a two piece suit you will pay a little over £650 (including VAT) – do not complain, Huntsmans up the road charge over £1000.

It is a pleasant amble from Savile Row down to St James's Street where you will find the rest of your bespoke kit – on the way you can call in at Hatchards Bookshop for an improving work or pick up anything from a new umbrella to a hunting crop at Swaine Adeney and Briggs. If you cut through the Piccadilly Arcade to Jermyn Street you can call in at your shirtmaker, most of whom sound like a golden brand of cigarette – New and Lingwood, Hilditch and Key or Turnbull and Asser.

Once in St James's, past White's at number 37, Boodle's at number 8 and Lewis's (for cigars) at number 19, you come to John Lobb, Bootmaker at Number 9. Of the many grand boot and shoemakers in London before the Hitler War, Lobb's is one of the very few survivors. The shoes are almost as durable as the firm, though one of Lobb's clients maintained that his hand-made shoes lasted a lifetime only because they were so uncomfortable that he went everywhere by taxi.

As you enter the shop, you are met first by the smell of leather, then by one of the assistants who is not only the fitter, but makes the lasts and your shoes as well. Samples of the Lobb range of boots and shoes are heaped up in a glass-fronted cupboard on the wall, but you can have anything you want – after all, you are the one who is paying. The style decided on, you choose the actual skin to be used – this can be anything from straight box-calf to the more exotic ostrich, kangaroo, lizard, snake or elephant hide (the trunks and ears of legally-culled tuskers only).

Once you have decided on the style and material, both feet are measured (do not forget to wear the weight of socks that you will use with your new boots or shoes, preferably without holes). As Lobb's have a full order book, you will have to wait for at least six months before your shoes are ready. There is no fitting, nor should there be need for one. Your beautiful, hand-made shoes will cost a minimum of £500, more for an exotic skin, plus around £100 for the trees. Slippers are cheaper, at a little over £400 plus the cost of whatever motif you choose (a coronet is £40). If you look after your shoes, they will last you a long time – shoes made forty years ago are still returned for repair.

Satisfied customers include:

a. the Duke of Wellington (the first) – boots only;
b. Her Majesty Queen Elizabeth II;
c. Guy Burgess.

When you finally pick up your shoes, there should be no need to ask your valet to break them in for you, as often happened 'in the old days'. You can guarantee that they will fit perfectly, unless of course they have used your great-grandfather's last by mistake.

Surveying the new reformed Parliament, the Duke of Wellington (the first) commented that he had 'Never seen so many damn'd

bad hats in m'life.' He was speaking not only metaphorically, since many of the new members had top hats of which he strongly disapproved as not being made by Mr Lock.

The Duke would doubtless consider that there are just as many bad hats in Parliament today, although it is the exception, rather than the rule, to see a hat on any man in London. The country, however, is a different matter, where the tweed cap and the *de rigueur* brown felt trilby (named after the du Maurier character) are essential for outside pursuits like shootin' and racin'. If you have an odd shaped head, you can, like the Duke of Wellington, have a hat made for you by James Lock – almost next door to Lobb's – at 6 St James's. It is now something of an extravagance, however, as one of their proprietary hats will, after a little attention, fit you perfectly.

The shop does not seem to have changed for two centuries. As you enter, you will be politely solicited as to your requirements. When you have told the assistant the type of hat you want, anything from a coke (after William Coke of Holkham who wore them; others would call them a bowler, after William Bowler of Southwark who made them), to something simple for the country, the assistant will bring out his *conformateur*. This is an ingenious device which measures the contours of your head and records them on a card. The experienced assistant can even hazard an informed guess as to your nationality – Americans have larger and longer heads than the British, Slav heads are rounder. It does not take long before your hat is steamed into shape and gold initials stamped inside. Once they have your card, you can re-order at will and your hats should fit. However, do not leave it more than a few decades between each visit as your head will change shape and shrink.

Satisfied Locks' customers include:

a. Lord Nelson;
b. The Duke of Edinburgh;
c. The Princess of Wales;
d. Lord Avon (better known as Anthony Eden);
e. Larry Hagman (better known as J R);
f. Mr Shifter, the Brook Bond Tea chimpanzee (coke size 5½).

If you were to go to St James's from your tailor in Savile Row by way of Bond Street, you would pass Sotheby's. Your amble might coincide with a visit from their watch expert, George Daniels.

## A WATCH FROM GEORGE DANIELS

If you want to know the time, ask a policeman or buy five litres of oil at your local petrol station and be given a quartz watch free – one will be as accurate as the other and good enough for most purposes. However, if it is perfection you are after, go to George Daniels. 'George Daniels is the finest watchmaker in the world,' says Teddy Beyer, a seventh generation Swiss watch master and, apart from a few jealous Swiss, no one who knows anything about horology would disagree. Mr Daniels' reputation rests on just sixteen watches, all unique, all undisputed masterpieces.

What sets this horological genius apart from every watchmaker since John Harrison (the maker of the first chronometer accurate enough for navigation in 1735) is his design, workmanship and artistry. The only reason Daniels makes another watch is to improve on the last or to add some new feature, such as a date, month and year dial for the next hundred years (including leap years). The workmanship is the best. Trusting nothing to anyone else, George Daniels himself makes every last piece in his workshop on the Isle of Man – the springs, wheels, even the screws, all accurate to a thousandth of a millimeter, all polished to a mirror finish. The jewels in the movement are also cut by him. What starts as a handful of inexpensive materials, literally a few pounds worth of gold, steel and diamond chips, after 2–2500 hours of his time ends up as a masterpiece.

The beauty of a Daniels' watch does not lie in the styling or the decoration of the case and face, but on his blend of high technology and aesthetic quality, combined with his own invented mechanism to enhance the development of the watch as a time-keeper. The proof of any watch is its accuracy, and George Daniels can boast 'zero variation from perfect time-keeping' when tested at the Royal Observatory.

What makes a George Daniels watch even more exclusive is that you can never commission one, and have to be extraordinarily lucky, not to say rich, to buy one. A handful of keen but anonymous collectors around the world possess one. He will only sell to those who can appreciate the intricate workings of his watches, and then only if he is bored with his latest watch. Upwards of £50,000 is needed to buy, as well as a promise that you will look after it, keep him informed of its progress and not lock it up in the bank as an investment.

You will have to wait a long time to buy the latest Daniels creation, a watch built to celebrate the centenary of Greenwich Mean Time and the dawn of the space age. No astronaut should be without it. On one side you can tell the time and date on earth – solar time based on the position of the sun. There is even a tiny pointer to show you how fast or slow the sun is when it crosses the Greenwich Meridian. On the other side you can tell the time in space – sidereal time based on the movement of the stars. There is also a stop watch that records on both timing systems, so you can time either your space walk or a child's sports day races. You will be fortunate to buy it for £150,000 (still cheaper than a French Impressionist) but you own the ultimate timepiece. 'The thing about a watch.' says George Daniels in his gruff voice, 'is that when it is finished there must be no indication that it has ever been made. It must just exist in perfection.'

## PORTRAIT PAINTING

Another pre-lunch pursuit is to sit for your portrait. The morning is the ideal time as the north light is the best to paint by and you should still be looking reasonably healthy. You will want to be painted because:

    a. you are carrying on a family tradition of portraiture that began with Holbein;
    b. you are so important that the walls of your company, bank, school/university, charity/husband/wife or lover can not be without your likeness. Some men have their wives painted when their marriages are under strain; it is a way of saying 'I love you', but without the bother;
    c. you are so beautiful and interesting that the artist *du jour* seeks your permission to paint you;

d. you think so highly of your physiognomy that you feel that it must be recorded for posterity.

First, the style of your portrait has to be decided. There are two major options – a straight portrait from an artist trained in the classical school, or a modern approach from an innovative painter. The innovatives enjoy a critical *réclame*, and the better known are considered a sound investment. However, the twisted emotions of the artist will more than likely overshadow your sweet features on the canvas – think of Francis Bacon on a bad day; is the Duchess of Devonshire *really* as green as Lucian Freud painted her?

Having decided on a classical portrait, to find a suitable painter is relatively simple. If you inquire at the Royal Society of Portrait Painters they will produce a list of their members, stating exactly what they charge. You can have a pastel for as little as £300 up to well over £5000 for a conversation piece plus £400 (plus VAT) per figure. The better known the artist, the busier they are. Among those with full order books:

a. Rodrigo Moynihan – one of the Grand Old Men of British art;
b. Carlos Sancha – a Royal portrait never did him any harm;
c. June Mendoza – a Royal portrait never did her any harm either, even if she does make you look like an illustration for a *Woman's Own* short story;
d. Richard Foster – more the mode of a stockbroker (he paints in a suit) than the talented painter he is;
e. the Hon. George Bruce, Hon. Sec. of the Royal Society of British Portrait Painters.

As a portrait painter, George J. D. Bruce comes highly recommended, if you can rely on the word of a former Speaker of the House of Commons, three Archbishops of Canterbury, a past Master of Trinity, a Lord Chief Justice *et al*.

Once you enter George Bruce's traditional artist's studio at 6 Pembroke Walk, at the grander end of Kensington, you enter a new and untried world where paint meets psychology. For the best results you should:

a. give as many sittings as possible – the busier the sitter, the more sittings they find time to give (studios are a place where you can not be contacted);

b. be comfortable – his studio looks like an antique chair shop with something to suit every shape and style;

c. be relaxed – it is a myth that you have to sit like a Buddha for three hours at a time.

Although George Bruce prefers to paint somewhat allegorical backgrounds, he will, if you ask him nicely, do a straight representation of your house and grounds, grouse moor, lodge, or whatever else you think suits you. Dress (or undress if female) is also optional unless it is out of character, like a suit of armour or angels' wings. Strong checks that resemble a Russian salad on a cheap charter flight are also out as they might frighten the portrait.

The actual sittings are restful and easy. You are lavishly entertained with conversation and anything between Earl Grey's tea and Lord Glenlivet's whisky. The artist should not be hurried and the portrait will take as many sittings as it takes to complete the picture. The reason why there are so many bad portraits of the Royal Family is that they do not have the time to devote to their many portrait painters, just four one-hour sittings, and the artist then has to make do with photographs.

When the day comes for you to hang your portrait, to the accompaniment of the best champagne and your friends, you will with luck be happier than:

a. Lady [Clementine] Churchill and Graham Sutherland;
b. John Singer Sargent and all his clients – 'every time I paint a portrait, I lose a friend';
c. Gertrude Stein and Picasso – after over eighty sittings he scratched out her head, declaring that he was unable to paint her. When he returned to the canvas some months later, he painted her from memory in one brief session. When their friends declared that the portrait was not at all like her, Picasso replied, 'Never mind, in time she will manage to look just like that';
d. Dorian Gray and Basil Halward.


## PORTRAIT PHOTOGRAPHY

Having a portrait photograph is very different from having your portrait painted. It is quicker, less taxing and less honest – the old cliché, the camera cannot lie, is far from the truth. There are as many society photographers as good portrait painters and, as in most occupations today, there is strong competition from within the aristocracy.

Coronets among the lenses:

a. Viscount Draynefleet – elder son and heir to Osbert Lancaster's Earl of Littlehampton. After being sacked from Eton and sent down from King's College, Cambridge, he went to London where he 'naturally gravitated to his sister's set in the King's Road where, having always been handy with a Kodak, he set himself up as a freelance photographer'. Unfortunately, being only a Viscount, and with a courtesy title at that, he found the competition of the Earls too great and abandoned photography for music;

b. The Earl of Lichfield (Patrick) – he will be delighted to fit you in between snapping the Royal Family, naked ladies for the Unipart calendar and mackintosh advertisements. Strongly resist his suggestion that he, too, should be in your photograph. Satisfied customers include: Sarah Lee, the Earl of Lichfield, Patrick Lichfield;

c. Viscount Moore (Derry) – son and heir to the Earl of Drogheda. Could well make more of your handsome interior than of your features;

d. The Earl of Snowdon (Tony) – Photographer Royal (although proceeds of any photographs of his ex-in-laws go to charity). Satisfied customers include: Raine Lewisham. Dissatisfied customers include: Agatha Christie;

e. Lord Settrington (Charles) – next but one Duke of Richmond and Gordon. May make more of your jewellery than you. Satisfied customers include Harvey Nichols;

f. Norman Parkinson – honorary peer (for coronet read topi). Much in demand, as his consummate skill can make beautiful women look even more beautiful and the dowdy acceptable. It would be no hardship if you had to go to him for your sitting – he lives in Tobago. Satisfied customers include: the Queen Mother and her daughters, Iman.

Whoever you choose to take your portrait, it would be an awful waste if immigration officers the world over were the only ones to see their work.

It would be agreeable to be able to lunch, following in the footsteps of Sam Johnson, George Selwyn and Sidney Smith, with latter-day literary giants. There are few such groups today, but a not too distant approximation would be lunch at the Beefsteak, a select club in Irving Street, by Leicester Square. From the outside it is indistinguishable from the many unsalubrious clubs in Soho, so much so that the place has been raided by the vice squad only to find a former Prime Minister, the Lord Chancellor, the Lord Chief Justice and the Archbishop of Canterbury placidly chomping their nursery fare.

A member once described it as 'a pleasant little club. The only qualification is that you've either got to be a peer who has learned to read and write or a journalist who has learned table manners.' At one time, to be elected you had to be a relation of God, and 'a damned close relation at that'. You will lunch, in order of your arrival, in the dining room at a long table. There, under a Gothic ceiling whose beams are in the shape of the Club's emblem, a grid-iron, you will consort with a mixture of peers, politicians, academics, writers and actors. Call the stewards and waiters 'Charles' whatever their baptismal name, a fine British eccentricity though one now deplored by some of the more democratic members. Also, forbear to give advice to your neighbour on any subject – you might find yourself in a similar position to the new member who told Rudyard Kipling how to write short stories. It is the one place where you can guarantee the quality of your fellow lunchers – you may also be lucky and have beefsteak, an Aberdeen Angus sirloin.

A somewhat less illustrious occasion, held in infinitely less salubrious surroundings, is the weekly lunch of the satirical magazine, *Punch*. You will be asked, initially, as one of two guests of the editor, Alan Coren, but later you may go as of right, should you become a 'Table Member'. Disabuse yourself of any illusion that you are about to enter a Dickensian panelled room with roaring fire and aproned servants. Instead, you will find yourself in a long, light and airy dining room (behind a door indistinguishable from any other office on the landing) the decor of which has Cunard overtones. If you arrive early you will have a chance to examine the framed cartoons on the walls, from Pont, Fougasse, and Shepherd (better remembered for illustrating *Winnie the Pooh*) up to present-day cartoonists. *Punch* has always parodied the views of the British middle classes, a view fostered by its editors: Malcolm Muggeridge, anti-Establishment in the 1950s; William Davies, brasher and 'go-getting'; and the present editor, Alan Coren, who has never worked anywhere else, a mirror of the 1980s.

Your fellow lunchers will be drawn from the staff and regular contributors plus a few outsiders. As his guest, you will sit to the right or left of Alan Coren, who presides over a table of anything up to twenty other hungry souls. The level of conversation depends on who is there – the cartoonists are easily recognizable as the most silent ones. Among the regulars, you may meet:

- a. Christopher Matthew – the urbane property writer;
- b. Michael Bywaters – Bunteresque listings editor; decked out in an Evelyn Waugh look-alike suit.
- c. Miles Kington – talking Franglais;
- d. Libby Purves – with luck without her baby;
- e. Clement Freud – mercifully without his bloodhound;
- f. Roy Hattersley – defender of the North of England, cricket and the Labour Party;
- g. Hunter Davies – another professional Northerner;
- h. Alan Brien – attends when hungry;
- i. Basil Boothroyd – the yellow Rolls Royce outside is his;
- j. Sheridan Morley – has to be witty with Noël Coward as his godfather;
- k. Melvyn Bragg – almost too busy to attend.

Other guests:

- a. the wittier members of the Royal Family;
- b. the wittier stars of stage and screen;
- c. the wittier columnists.

To go with the wit, there is the adequate British fare that you would expect in such a British institution – roast beef or lamb. The cheese board is highly recommended. The drink is good, with a different wine with each course, and brandy and cigars (avoid the poor pun '*Punch* drunk'), before Alan Coren bangs his gavel on the table to make a short speech on the contents of the next issue.

If you are a *very* special guest, you will be invited to carve your initials on 'the *Punch* Dining Table'. This is a great honour, as it is generally reserved for the longest standing contributors – writers and cartoonists – since the magazine's founding in 1841. Your place mat is a facsimile of the table below the white damask cloth. Only five outsiders have become 'table members':

a. the Duke of Edinburgh;
b. the Prince of Wales;
c. Princess Anne;
d. James Thurber;
e. Mark Twain, who was invited to sign but declined saying that two-thirds of William Makepeace Thackeray's initials would suffice for him.

A *Punch* lunch should not be confused with a *Private Eye* lunch, held every fortnight in a Soho pub – the Coach and Horses. You will be asked by the editor, Richard Ingrams, not for your wit or intelligence, but in the hope that you will divulge information for the next issue. Unless you have a particular score to settle or are partial to steak and chips, token MPs, rude landlords and cheap wine, you will do better to give their lunch a wide berth. There, the only carving is done in the back.

If you wish to observe the British parodying themselves, then it would be better to repair to one of the famous London Clubs. *White's*, the oldest of all, is self-consciously grand, although some would agree with Swift who dubbed it the 'common *rendezvous* of infamous sharpers and noble cullies'. It has more than its fair share of members drawn from the pages of Burke's Peerage. It would be invidious to tot up the total acreage owned by the members – the Duchy of Cornwall is pretty large for a start. At White's, the food is fair, with a better wine cellar, the staff loyal and needfully discreet, and the club itself, with its five-year waiting list (longer if they do not like you), the epitome of all that makes it the envy of the club world. Also in St James's is Boodle's, another venerable establishment where there are now women members with their own dining room (better food than up front) and Brooks's, opposite Boodle's, the great Whig club – forbear to make jokes about the erstwhile cockroaches in the kitchen, they are uncalled for as the food is really quite good. Buck's (the prototype of Brat's in Evelyn Waugh's *Handful of Dust*) is another good lunching spot, as is the Turf – nod affectionately to Grace, the head porter who has been there for over fifty years (he began at the age of sixteen washing the members' loose change). The Garrick, as its name implies, specializes in the stage and actors *manqués* (barristers and judges), with a fair smattering of literary talent.

In any of these clubs, if you go in on your own you can join the centre table and are then compelled to converse with your neighbours. Whereas you can, all too often, draw a short straw, you can also strike lucky and find yourself next to the very person whom you have always wanted to meet.

Many of the London clubs have a strong gambling background and, with nothing better to do, you can spend the afternoon happily playing backgammon or snooker – some clubs have their own version of the game, like White's and the Turf who call theirs 'slosh'.

## LUNCH IN THE CITY

'I love merchant banking,' said one City man. 'It's so entrepreneurial: his gun in his hand, my knife in his back.' The City of London is a square mile jungle of banks and discount houses, of Lloyds and other insurance brokers, of Exchanges (Stock, Baltic, Royal, London Metal), the Mansion House for the Lord Mayor and the ninety-three Livery Companies that all have trade titles – Mercers, Fishmongers and the like – but there the resemblance to trade ends. As much an institution as the Bank of England is the traditional City Lunch.

All City firms of any note have their own dining rooms in which to entertain themselves, their clients and anyone else whom they wish to impress. The quality of the food and certainly of the wine (if any) has generally sunk to the level of the canteen. Perhaps this is for the better, the thought of your fees being turned into *Haut Brion* '55 for your broker's lunch so that he could act even more inefficiently on your behalf in the afternoon can only have been galling.

However, there are still a few venues where you can find

genial surroundings, interesting guests, adequate food and an exceptional cellar. One sought-after invitation is to lunch with the Governor and Court of Directors of the Bank of England. Your invitation will come from the present Governor, Robin Leigh-Pemberton, and your fellow guests will be drawn from the hierarchy of the City, members of both Houses of Parliament, the captains of industry, an ambassador or, as at the Queen's lunches at Buckingham Palace, a few others of note in other spheres to make it interesting. After a good lunch (the Governor is something of a connoisseur of the better clarets), he in theory might award you the greatest honour of the Bank of England – your own private bank account with the 'Old Lady of Threadneedle Street'. Although those who work for the Bank and past Governors have their accounts there, it is extremely rare for an outsider to do so, unless after a very distinguished career in the City like that of the Chairman of the Stock Exchange. Not even members of the Royal Family bank there; they go to Coutts. You need not be embarrassed if you are not rich; all you need is £200 and they will open the account and give you a smart chequebook and a banker's card – yellow in colour – so that you can cash your cheques anywhere. As a bank, it offers no better service than any other in the high street and you may find that your local store looks on your cheques as Monopoly money, but it will impress those who are really in the know.

Another smart invitation comes from the Lord Mayor, to lunch at the Mansion House. Hope for a small, private lunch – to be one of six hundred is hardly exclusive, however imperial the setting. For real money-talk and the best lunches, however, you should be invited by one of the discount houses; try Smith St Aubyn or King and Shaxson, who really do well for their guests. Stockbrokers' dining rooms used to be good but have now largely substituted beer for claret to go with something similar to nursery food. De Zoete and Bevan, Messels, Laurie Milbank, Rowe and Pilman are still good; if it is advice on your portfolio that you are after, try the butlers – they keep their ears open, their mouths shut and remain sober.

City restaurants are generally to be avoided, they are expensive and crowded between noon and four o'clock in the afternoon. The City clubs are grim. There is one place to lunch where you

can combine adequate food with the very best wines and that is as the guest of the City firm of wine merchants, Green's Ltd, in their private dining rooms above their shop behind the Royal Exchange. You will be taken up to an unpretentious dining room by a pretty secretary where you will meet your hosts – Richard Parsons, a man with the air of a popular prep school master who coached the colts XI (which he was) and Frank Waldron, the one with the bearing of a captain of the Scots Guards (which he was). As you tuck into their house champagne you meet your fellow guests. They are a varied lot, drawn mostly from the City, being the partners responsible for the wine buying in their firm's dining room and therefore more genial than the partner in charge of stationery, possibly the owner of the *petit domaine* near Avignon where the *Chateauneuf-du-Pape* you may be drinking comes from, an Arab Prince, a minor Royal, a famous restauranteur, a wine writer and the like. The food is unspectacular but a wonderful foil for the wines and the conversation. Talk revolves round wine, country pursuits and rowing.

At the end of lunch the competition is hot to guess the vintage of the port. If you are extremely lucky, you may even have to guess the century of the Armagnac. You will be asked to sign the visitors' book and, as they record the wines you have drunk at lunch on the same page, you can check what you have been drinking, just in case you did not recognize them. Whatever else you do, remember what your grandfather told you about mixing port and brandy. If you forget, your lunch at Green's Ltd may be remembered for other reasons.

Depending on the length of your lunch, it is not long before it is time for tea. Like breakfast, heavy teas are best left to the country, and the weekend at that, but a delicate tea does help separate the alcohol from lunch and preprandial drinks.

## TEA AT THE HOUSE OF LORDS

To an outsider viewing the system of British government, the House of Lords must seem the greatest anachronism of all. In it you will find a splendid collection of octagenarian earls with patrician noses, eloquent hereditary peers on the opposition benches and an odd assortment of life peers, created after a lifetime of service to the country or to the Prime Minister, some looking like Holbein portraits of those who founded new noble houses on the proceeds of the dissolution of the monasteries. The House of Lords is a great British institution. As with all great British institutions, the British do not ask themselves how or why it works but merely rejoice in the fact that it does. The House of Lords has been working – more or less – for nigh on nine hundred years.

One way to observe this archaic system at first hand is to take tea in the House of Lords dining room. It is best to be invited by an elderly hereditary peer, as he will be able to give you his time and point out the more interesting of his colleagues. You will be asked to present yourself at the Peers' Entrance at Whitehall, 'opposite the statue of King George V' – in fact Westminster Abbey is bigger and more easily recognized. Brush past the policeman with a 'footman's nod' (cf Weekend, page 53) and present yourself to the beadle, immaculate in his white tie and gilt chain of office, who will fill out your bright green card marked 'Peer's Guest House of Lords'. He will take your coat – do not be tempted to hang it up yourself on a spare peg, all members have their own hook and, although your coat may well be smarter than theirs, the intrusion will not be appreciated. Make your way upstairs along red carpets (the Commons' carpet is green) and down a long corridor to the Peers' Guests' Room which is actually a bar – there are no licensing laws in either House so members can have a drink at any hour of the day or night that the House is sitting. There you will meet your host, who will take you across the corridor to the Peers' Dining Room. Avoid the temptation to go through to the far room, the 'Peers Only' dining room (unless of course you are of their ranks) – your invasion will be greeted as if you were Charles I or Lloyd George with one of his budgets. Your end is just as nice, although you sit under a portrait of Lord Byron rather than a shifty-looking Henry VII.

Little has changed in the decor of Augustus Pugin's original Peers' Dining Room of 1847 – there is the same design of wallpaper printed from the original blocks, the carpet is woven to the same pattern and colour. Even the chairs have been copied and replaced as they wore out. The only sign of the times is the paper tablecloth and napkins they use for tea.

The tea itself is a perfectly adequate affair, the China tea being better than the Indian, the toasted tea cakes far better than the cream cakes and buns. In the House of Lords you can at least guarantee the calibre of the company, the singers if not the song – keep your back to the wall for the best peer-spotting.

When you leave, ask the beadle to hail you a taxi. Most likely, when the cabby drops you off at your house he will touch his forelock with a 'thank you m'lord'. All the world knows that all the world loves a lord. You will not be at home for long. Around 6 o'clock life begins anew. Your day could advance into one of many directions. If you are not going to a private drinks party, there are two that are at least semi-private – the publishers' book launch and the art gallery opening.

## THE BOOK LAUNCH

Despite the claims of the Americans, who think that they invented the novel, or the fact that the French hold the record number of Nobel Prizes for literature, the British believe that their writing is incomparably the best. Today, in the absence of the grand literary salons, literary life in England is best observed at the interminable succession of parties given by publishers to launch themselves and their books, in particular during the publishing season from September to November.

Unfortunately, the quality of the parties has suffered from the quantity given. As they swallow *vin plonque* and nibble on a Twiglet, the senior literati lament the passing of the champagne and smoked salmon of the old days. However, there are still a few intimate and illuminating book launch parties to be found, the ultimate being a dinner in a private dining room (better than the Coffee Room – the main dining room) at the Garrick. Publishers like to spread their parties around, however, particularly if they can thus highlight the theme of the book being launched – the Crush Bar at Covent Garden for opera and ballet books, the elephant house at London Zoo for animal books (beware of zoo parties, the publicity girl's scent is generally worse than anything she is trying to conceal with it).

Publishers' party pieces:

a. Quartet – to Naim Attallah, the party is more important than the book, which means a lavish spread. The launch is also a chance for him to show off the beauty, breeding and intelligence of his bevy of personal assistants;

b. Weidenfeld – Lord 'George's' flat on the Embankment overlooking the Thames is the top venue to show off his guests. You can gauge the importance of the book by your fellow guests – if Lord Wilson of Rievaulx, Lady Falkender or Lady Antonia Fraser are there then the publisher deems it a serious addition to his list;

c. John Murray – hope that their party is held in their offices so that you can inspect Bernini's bust of Lord Byron, who, like Lord Weidenfeld, believed that 'a *live* lord must be worth

*two* dead', and a rather surprising lock of hair from Lady Caroline Lamb.

Whichever publisher and wherever the venue, you will meet roughly the same people:

a.  the author/authoress (allegedly the raison d'être of the party) and his/her friends and friendly family – often literary luminati like Lord and Lady Longford (Frank and Elizabeth) and their children Thomas Pakenham, Antonia Pinter *vide* Fraser above) and Rachel Billington; Kingsley Amis and his son Martin; Elizabeth Jane Howard and her step-son Martin; Margaret Drabble and Michael Holroyd. The Royal Family are now all rushing into print – the Duke of Edinburgh, the

Prince of Wales, Prince Andrew, Prince Edward, the Duke of Gloucester, his mother, Princess Michael of Kent, to drop but a few – they do not personally launch their books – they have no need;

b. agents – a range of ten percenters always much in evidence;
c. other publishers, particularly those from paperback houses who are invariably affable to all as they are in the bidding for the rights of the book being launched. They generally sound as if they have come from an aviary, menagerie or kennel;
d. booksellers – the better the party the classier the bookseller; little to choose between John Saumarez-Smith of Heywood Hill, John Sandoe of himself, Peter Giddy of Hatchards, Charles Leigh-Pemberton of Truslove and Hanson (even although it *is* part of W. H. Smith's);
e. literary editors from the dailies and magazines – as there are so many launch parties during the 'season' you can gauge the class of your party by those who turn up;
f. gossip columnists – usually a sprinkling hanging around for *bons mots*.

As you leave the party to go on to dinner, with luck having met a famous author or authoress, do not forget to pick up one of the promotional copies of the book and have it signed by the author. Neither publisher nor author will be pleased about the lost sale, but then you can not satisfy everybody.

## THE GALLERY OPENING

'The trouble with galleries', complained Oscar Wilde, 'is that there are either so many people that you cannot see the pictures or there are so many pictures that you cannot see the people.' Nevertheless, private views at both public and commercial galleries, if chosen with care, can be artistically rewarding as well as entertaining.

As most of the major exhibitions at the important London galleries are sponsored by large corporations, it is best to go on the sponsors' evening. Not only will you be given champagne (the alternative is cheap wine that has probably never seen a grape), but you will mingle with every expert in the particular field of the exhibition. Anything to do with Italy tends to produce their Embassy and a particularly glamorous set. If you leave your viewing to the Friends' preview of whichever gallery it is, then you are in for a pay bar and a crush – Friends have friends, and friends of Friends have even more friends, like Rabbit's relations or fleas.

To be sure of your invitation to the opening night party, you should be on the private mailing list of the directors of each gallery – the most important being Sir Hugh Casson of the Royal Academy (for the Summer Exhibition) and Professor Alan Bowness of the Tate. Time spent in impressing these is never wasted.

Private views of important exhibitions are few and far between, but the commercial art galleries, and occasionally the fine art auction houses, have a succession of private views to launch their exhibitions. Since the smarter private views have largely taken over from drinks parties as meeting places in London, it is there that you meet your friends, not to mention the artist (if alive). As in all things, you have to choose your venue carefully as, in the fifteen or so openings a week, only a few are exclusive.

With a few notable exceptions, you should stay within that square mile roughly bounded by St James's, King Street, up Bury Street to New Bond Street and ending at Cork Street. If you are a serious buyer, you will be asked to the preview of the preview – no gallery owner would dream of letting you loose on his competitors. If you are a possible buyer, a respectable friend of the artist, or have signed the visitors' book enough times, you will be sent an embossed invitation to the private view. Depending on the time you arrive, you will find an amazing assortment of people, falling mainly into two camps:

a. The early pre-prandialists – those on their way home from their offices or going to the theatre;
b. The later pre-prandialists – those looking in on their way out to dinner. Dress ranges from black tie and long dresses to the open toed sandals of the critics of the more *avant garde* art magazines.

Once you have signed the visitors' book (to assure your next invitation), you gravitate towards the people and the pictures in the gallery. Galleries are differentiated by their hospitality as much as by the type of pictures they sell. You will find:

a. champagne at Partridge (Fine Arts) and Wildenstein, both of New Bond Street; Lefèvre, Bruton Street; Colnaghi, Old Bond Street and the Redfern Gallery in Cork Street;
b. drinkable wine at the Maclean Gallery, St George Street; Anthony d'Offay, Dering Street and Oliver Swann in Walton Street;
c. tea at Knoedler-Kasmin of Cork Street (three to six only).

The better the private view, the more it is like a drinks party. Conversation is general although it occasionally relates to the pictures – if you can see them. The more expensive the pictures, the higher the percentage of Americans among the guests. Try not to wince visibly when you hear in a Texan drawl:

a. 'Are you the artist?' to the young gallery assistant or 'Are you the artist's daughter?' to the twinset-and-pearls gallery secretary, at an exhibition of Old Masters;
b. 'I buy Bonnards mostly as they go so well with my new wallpaper';
c. 'I don't know anything about art, but I know what I like.'

As you know about both art and what you like, you can express your opinions loudly. You may even find someone to listen to you. If you do not like the pictures at all, you will certainly find someone to listen to you. In that case, insist that the picture:

a. is 'a dog' – not one of Rafael Valls' canine exhibitions in his Cadogan Gallery, but dreadful in every way;
b. has been skinned – has been overcleaned;
c. is somewhat of a 'pastiche' – a way of saying without fear of slander that the picture is a fake.

Whether you like the pictures (and/or the people) a good private view will set you up adequately for dinner.

## DINNER

There has always been a rich choice of places to dine out in London, whether in restaurants (mostly metropolitan French, provincial Italian or back-street Cypriot passing as Greek) or at one of the better clubs. The latter tends to be rather gloomy unless eating with a specialized dining club. Here the British excel, as with:

a. The Dilettanti, who meet once a quarter at Brooks's under the aegis of Sir Brinsley Ford: for grandees who own a collection of old masters, and savants who know whether the old masters are genuine and how much they would fetch at auction. Dress is formal save for the president who is liable to appear in a red cloak and comic hat;

b. The Sublime Society of Beefsteaks, who meet at the Beefsteak (and other venues) once a month under the aegis of Count Nicolai Tolstoi: for those who could slip back easily into a squirearchical eighteenth century. Dress is generally eccentric and much in keeping with the eighteenth century;

c. The Shikar Club, who meet annually at the Savoy Hotel under the aegis of Lord Lovat: for those who have a penchant for the peerage and a love of killing big game. Dress, as for the grander hunting parties in the field, is black tie with a predominance of stiff wing collars.

Whatever the delights of eating out, it rarely compares with dining at your, or better still, someone else's home. There are still a few grand dinner parties given in London. The smarter the dinner the further ahead you will be asked and the heavier the embossing on the engraved invitation. A scribbled message at the bottom might give a hint as to who will be there – 'to entertain the Italian Ambassador and Signora Catiati' – or an idea as to the occasion – 'to celebrate John's release from Ford Open Prison'.

You will be asked at 8 o'clock for 8.15 which means you should turn up at some time between the two. The invitation will also specify if it is 'black tie' (as it is for a Royal TV dinner eaten on your knees). Having negotiated what seems like an amalgam of the best stands at the Chelsea Flower Show, the butler, resident or imported, will show you to your hosts' drawing room and will return with your drink, seemingly without having left the room. If your host is generous it could be champagne, Krug 1969. In the drawing room, you will meet the other guests – today, London dinner parties seldom sit down more than eighteen. When dinner is ready, the butler will whisper in your hostess's ear – gongs are for the country and 'Dinner is served' shouted by the butler is for bad B movies.

Fortunately, strict protocol is a relic of the past and apart from the guests of honour, if there are any, who sit to the right of the host and hostess however dull they may be, your neighbours will at least have been chosen with care. Conversation at dinner is as important as the food and is usually better remembered. It may even follow:

a. Oscar Wilde, who thought that 'when people talk to us about others they are usually dull. When they talk to us about themselves they are nearly always interesting';
b. Baltasar Gracian, who believed that 'if to talk to oneself when alone is folly, it must be doubly unwise to listen to oneself in the presence of others';
c. Liza Kirk, who maintained that 'a gossip is one who talks to you about others; a bore is one who talks to you about himself; and a brilliant conversationalist is one who talks to you about yourself';
d. Montaigne, who steadfastly held that 'for table talk, I prefer the pleasant and witty before the learned and the grave; in bed, beauty before goodness'.

Dinner over, one glance from the hostess is generally enough to move the women out of the dining room and leave the men behind – a British habit frowned upon by women and foreigners alike. Little has changed since the eighteenth century when Rochefoucauld wrote, 'a gentleman can not make good conversation without the company of ladies and nowhere is this better demonstrated than in London when at dinner the ladies retire and the gentlemen are expected to converse for a further three hours.' Your hostess, however, would not tolerate three hours.

When the men are finally united with the women in the drawing room for some cold coffee, you will find that you have been joined by those who have 'come in after dinner'. The men will be in varying states of dress with their female equivalents:

a. white tie – those who have managed to escape from a dinner at their City livery guild;

b. black tie – those who have escaped from another dinner party and hope to find yours more amusing;
c. suits – those who have supped in front of their favourite serial on television and dragged themselves out;
d. jeans – those who have been refused admission at Annabels and so come on from Tramp (no 's').

If there are members of the Royal Family present, you can not leave before they do which may be very late indeed. It is unwise to solicit a lift home from them, nor will your hostess thank you if you take the prettiest girl/man away to Annabels or Aspinalls.

The sooner you write your thank-you letter, the shorter it can be. If it arrives with flowers, your invitation to the next party is doubly guaranteed.

## DINING AT OXFORD

If you were to tire of London social life, there is the stimulation of a dinner at High Table to be had at any of the grander colleges at Oxford or Cambridge. Both Oxford and Cambridge, jointly known as Oxbridge, are fifty or so miles from London in distance, up to eight hundred years away in time, but at the heart of the metropolis by every other standard.

Though Oxford has traditionally favoured the Arts and Cambridge the Sciences, rivalry exists between them on a sporting rather than an academic plane – the Boat Race, the Varsity [rugger] Match, polo, tiddlywinks, even the proper way to punt (Oxford punt from the front end, standing inside the boat, Cambridge punt from the platform at the back). They are united, however, in that they both consider themselves infinitely superior to all other universities, regardless of the latters' venerability, academic achievement or sporting prowess.

Harvard may be cleverer, the University of California may make more row, and Edinburgh produce the best distillers and brewers, but Oxbridge are still top because of their:

a. old buildings – two of the finest collections of architecture in the country in the most beautiful of settings – the Backs at Cambridge or the view of Tom Tower from Christ Church meadows, Magdalen Deer Park, the wild flowers (including the rare snakeshead fritillaries) in Addison's on a May morning, the Cherwell flowing past Oscar Wilde's rooms . . .;

b. old dons – there are more grey beards to the acre than anywhere else in the academic world. Being the best, they naturally attract and keep the best;

c. old habits – where modern is nineteenth century and tradition rules supreme. Nikita Khrushchev once asked the President of Magdalen why the choir was singing in the chapel, to which the president replied, 'Because it has done so for five hundred years';

d. old pride – 'My name translates as the son of God,' blushingly admitted a Japanese prince on his arrival at Oxford. 'Ah yes, you will find the sons of many distinguished men here,' unblushingly replied the president of his college.

Some colleges are smarter than others. Generally, the better the undergraduates do academically (academic achievement is still felt to be not quite British, certainly not quite the Very Best of British), the less they gain from what *really* matters at Oxbridge like:

a. learning to drink good wine – at the elite dining clubs like the Grid or the Pitt;

b. learning to spend money – the 'Brideshead' set are still in evidence although they spend most of their time in London;

c. preparing for country life – the Bullingdon rowdies rally to their point-to-point, hunt with their drag hounds, even beagle;

d. behaving badly – as with Hilaire Belloc's John Vavassour de Quentin Jones, 'Like many of the Upper Class, He liked the sound of Broken Glass'. Oxbridge undergraduates still enjoy baying for broken glass, wrecking rooms (other people's) and restaurants;

e. gaining confidence – learning that it is possible to get everything you want at Oxbridge and therefore, by the same token, it is possible to get everything you want in later life.

To experience the best that senior as opposed to undergraduate Oxbridge has on offer, dine at one of their colleges. Again, colleges vary greatly as to what they can offer:

a. All Souls for all that is best. Academic patter is so well honed as to be incomprehensible to the outsider, as is the wit of the senior fellows like the Lords Wilberforce, Hailsham and Sherfield, Sir Keith Joseph or the younger politician, the Hon. William Waldegrave. Dessert and coffee served in the Codrington after dinner is equally memorable;
b. Peterhouse, Cambridge for the best food;
c. Magdalen, Oxford for the best conversation;
d. Christ Church, Oxford for the best wine;
e. Trinity, Cambridge for the best way to catch pneumonia.

Christ Church, written Ch Ch and known as the House, has always considered itself the grandest college at Oxford and is still the heartland of titled undergraduates – though the days when they wore golden tassels on their mortar boards and were exempt from exams are long gone.

You can be invited to High Table by any of the dons when they dine in Hall during term-time and if you are a graduate of any college you can from time to time attend a gaudy during the vacations. A Christ Church gaudy, from the latin *gaudeamus igitur*, therefore let us rejoice, is an occasion where you meet your contemporaries to give heartfelt thanks that Christ Church was, Christ Church remains, and that you were up at Christ Church.

If you are dining in term-time, present yourself to the bowler-hatted porter at the main gates under Tom Tower at five past seven. As he escorts you across Tom Quad to the Common Room, the bell, Great Tom, will strike seven times – Christ Church time is five minutes slow. Over a glass of dry sherry in the Common Room you will meet many of the dons who are dining in that night – you may be lucky and have Professor Hugh Lloyd-Jones, Regius Professor of Greek and archetypal Oxford don; Peter Oppenheimer, Senior Censor and presenter of 'File on 4', or Professor Sir Dimitri Obolensky, who, being a Russian prince, is appropriately Professor of Russian and Balkan History. The Dean might possibly be there as well – he is head of the college as well as Dean of the Cathedral, the chapel of Christ Church. If the Dean finds you important, interesting or attractive, or any combination of the three, he will invite you to sit on his right at dinner. Call him 'Mr Dean', even though he is the Very Reverend E. W.

Heaton. The head butler will hand the Dean his mortar board when it is time to go up to dinner. Whoever you are, do not precede him up the spiral staircase to the Great Hall and the High Table. The undergraduates will all be seated and half way through their dinner and will only rise when grace is read by one of the scholars.

You can not guarantee the quality of the food, usually adequate but nothing special, nor of the conversation probably relaxed for your benefit, but you can look forward to, and drink the finest wines from the dons' exceptional cellar. The wine served is commensurate with the importance of the dinner, but even the everyday drinking wine is superior to the best vintages of many other colleges. Dinner over, the scholar will read a long latin grace and, if it is a special occasion like a gaudy, the Dean will propose the toast, 'The Queen, the visitor of Christ Church'. Coffee and dessert are taken in the Common Room where the Curator of the Common Room, the most senior fellow present, seats the dons and their guests. At Christ Church, dessert is an exceptional port, Madeira or Sauterne, with fruit, cigars and snuff, and a dish of sweets. Like the port, the conversation is rich and vintage.

When you leave at the end of the evening and re-enter the real world, you leave with just a taste of what at least believes itself to be the Very Best of British. Perhaps it even is.

## ANNABELS

If very expensive fare, a long waiting list for membership, efficient staff and elegant decor are the criteria for a good London club, then Annabels, the nightclub in Berkeley Square, is streets ahead of many of those antique Establishment clubs, with their falling membership, dingy rooms and shuffling staff. But then, you can hardly include Annabels among the clubs in your entry in *Burke's*, *Debrett's* or *Who's Who*. To its habitués, who dine or go in after dinner, it has more the feel of a private house than a nightclub. It is still considered by members, would-be members and even those who dislike nightclubs at any price, as the ultimate nightclub.

Annabels' secret formula lies with its founder, Mark Birley (the club was named after his former wife, Lady Annabel Goldsmith).

This latter-day Patronius converted what was once the cellars, kitchens and subterranean garden of Number 44 Berkeley Square, into a series of interconnecting rooms. The lighting is soft, the chairs and sofas of extreme comfort, and the carpet tartan (green and red). A splendid collection of pictures graces the walls (note the predominance of dogs) by the likes of Landseer, Augustus John and Charles Burton Barber. A large buddha dominates the small room off the outside bar – the mind boggles at the conversation it has heard from the wide sofa below. You can stay by the outer bar or lounge on the sofas opposite, or you can go through to the inner bar before you dine in near total darkness, tables dimly lit by polished brass lamps with dark green shades. There you are shielded from your neighbours by slim stanchions, and, in return for a king's ransom, you eat well and drink better. At the end of the dining room is the dance floor – like the sofas, the music is soft. You can also take the private dining room, in the wine cellar, for thirteen of your closest friends where you will dine, looked after by the butler, George, amongst famous vintages, racked from floor to ceiling.

The staff are a vital part of Annabels' success. They arrived as the painters moved out and, with a few additions, have stayed ever since. To the man (and woman), they evoke a long departed era of dedicated service.

The brigade:

a. as you arrive, you will be greeted by Nando, the doorman, the alpha and omega of Annabels – he is the man who takes and returns your car. He was once described as 'the only doorman this side of St Peter's who prefers polite English guests to big-tipping but arrogant foreigners'. Younger Old Harrovian members remember his son as deputy head boy at school;

b. Mabel, who reigns over the ladies' cloakroom, is a much revered institution. She is good for gossip, aspirins, a handkerchief and a dry shoulder;

c. Sidney, who manages the outside bar, remembers what you drink and respectfully suggests that high spirits have their limits;

d. John presides over the inner bar and never forgets a face –

in and out of Annabels. Longchamps for the Prix de l'Arc de Triomphe and York Races are a speciality where he receives his more favourite clients;

e. Louis, the Manager, Freddie, the Assistant Manager, and Joseph the Sommelier, the maître d's and the spirit of the restaurant;

f. Ted and Eddie – the receptionists who never forget a member and always recognize a non-member. They welcome and dispatch with the same blend of respectful firmness, which strikes home whichever side of the fence you are on.

In the end, a club is only as good as its members. At Annabels there are a little over six thousand who come from all over the world, though they are mostly British. Although their background and breeding is diverse, they have one thing in common, whatever else they may do in other more ephemeral clubs or restaurants, their behaviour and dress befits the surroundings. By never lowering its standards, Annabels can safely be classed as the Very Best of British.

## TRANSPORT

Not wholly essential to London life is your car. It attracts :

a. unnatural substances – clamps;

b. unnatural curves – your wings rearranged by over-zealous taxis;

c. unnatural lines – called 'jealousy lines' and added to the sides by the key element of a certain brand of football supporter;

d. unnatural attention of the law, in the form of the breathalizer – one *roué* actually left to live in the South of France, declaring that 'London was impossible as it was illegal to drive after 10.30 in the morning.'

However, when you wish to leave London for your weekend, your holiday in Scotland or your chosen sport, then you will need some transport of your own – the trains used to be a good substitute but since James Sherwood has bought up all the decent carriages for his Orient Express, British Rail is hardly exclusive any more.

'Glorious, stirring sight . . . the poetry of motion. The real way to travel. The only way to travel. Here today – in next week tomorrow.' Had Mr Toad, that connoisseur of the automobile, been alive today, he could not have resisted any of the Aston Martin range. Although the horn does not actually go 'poop poop' (their twin windtone horns have a rather sophisticated town or raucous country note) he would have admired every other feature of this most British of cars.

Those thoroughly nice people at the Aston Martin showroom in Sloane Street will not be so vulgar as to speak of mechanical niceties like BHPs, torque, compression ratios or the like, other than to say that the car goes very quickly – over twice the legal speed limit – is extremely comfortable and has a Falstaffian thirst for petrol. As the owner of the latest Aston Martin Lagonda, you will join the ranks of those latter-day Mr Toads, a band of rich and discerning automobilists. Your Lagonda motor car will be:

a. exclusive by number – Aston Martin make only ten Lagondas a month and there is a waiting list of around six months. Most go for export to America and the Middle East, so there are few on the roads in Britain;
b. exclusive by design – good, solid no-nonsense British lines that are still exciting even though they have changed little for years. Also, you do not need to be a legless child or a dachshund on castors to sit in the back seats;
c. exclusive by build – solid like a tank with a proper old-fashioned coach-built body of aluminium. As with your suits, your engine is hand-built. If you re-order, you can ask for the same mechanic, as his nameplate is fixed to the engine;
d. exclusive by ownership – your Lagonda is a mark of quality, not a status symbol, so (unlike Rolls Royce drivers) you will not be mistaken for
    i. a pop-star
    ii. a property dealer on the make or on the way down
    iii. your book-maker financed by you
    iv. the driver trying harder to look like any of the above, while returning the hired Roller to Avis.

Satisfied customers include:
  a. HRH the Prince of Wales;
  b. the Duke of Westminster;
  c. Rowan Atkinson;
  d. HRH The Sultan of Brunei, who has a complete set.

Another of the pleasures of buying a Lagonda, as opposed to a Rolls Royce or a similar 'class' car, is that you do not have to deal with an obsequious pin-striped salesman in an expensive showroom that resembles a secondary greenhouse at Kew Gardens. Just stroll into their showroom, and in no time at all a superior salesman will sign you up with the model and colour of your choice. Lagondas are not cheap at £69,994.66, or you can go for the special version at £105,000 (with enough change to buy six packets of Polo mints). This has a special body and other obvious necessities, such as a television, video recorder and drinks cupboard, all built and fitted by Aston Martin Tickford.

There are few extras – air-conditioning, wireless and number plates are free. However, you might treat yourself to a set of Aston Martin luggage of birds-eye Maple and pig-skin at £4500 for a set of four suitcases. If you are an odd shape, you can have your seats specially made to fit your frame – if re-ordering, remember to state change of wife/husband/lover as they keep meticulous records.

As you drive off smoothly in supreme leather comfort, the huge boot filled with enough Aston Martin luggage for the Grand Tour, spare a thought for that 'traffic queller of the road', Mr Toad, for fortunately, there are not many of you still about.

## FLYING MACHINES

If Leonardo da Vinci had known what a difference the helicopter would make to life, he might have devoted more of his time and talents to developing his invention. He would doubtless have been proud of the way things are shaping up in the West Country, where Westland make Britain's only helicopter. The advantages of owning and flying such a machine are obvious – the Duke of Edinburgh (speaking *only* of helicopters) 'finds it an amusing business sort of wriggling your way in, and plonking down where you want to plonk down.' It is also a relatively simple operation to acquire this senior form of transport as, at only £2,000,000 (allow another £500,000 for extras), those nice people at Westland are only too pleased to sell you the latest in their range, the Westland 30.

Your first approach should be by letter, preferably not on the writing paper of St Andrew's Hospital, Northamptonshire (by appointment to the more deranged of the aristocracy), so that they can see you are a genuine buyer. It is best to call on them in London; turn left out of the Turf (Club) and they are practically next door in Carlton Gardens (they are also handy for Farlows, the fishing tackle shop). Alternatively, you can go to their factory to see the machine in construction, but then you would be blinded by science. Far better that they come to you. Before you actually buy, you should make sure that:

a. you can 'plonk' down in your garden (seduce your neighbours, if you have any, with offers of free rides as, although quiet inside, choppers are noisy beasts outside);
b. you can make it to wherever you are stalking, shooting, fishing or weekending in one hop at a speed of 120 m.p.h.;
c. you have enough room for your family, polo sticks, guns, picnic hampers, hat boxes and sundry luggage;
d. you can afford the running costs – around £500 per hour (plus incidental expenses like the pilot's salary), total – say – £75,000 per annum.

Having decided that the Westland 30 is for you, the next stage is to have the cabin fitted out. Unlike its American rivals, your helicopter is large and roomy, and, as with London cabs, the roof is high enough for you to sit down without removing your top hat (a feature of this chopper is that you do not have to duck under the rotor blades; it would be prudent, nevertheless, to remove your top hat as you exit). The standard executive interior is all right if you are a standard executive, but better by far to have it tailored to your own impeccable taste. Most interior designers would whirl at the chance as yours will be, after all, the only privately-owned Westland in the country. A good choice of designer would be Melissa Wyndham, by appointment to the aristocracy.

Should a helicopter not fill all your needs, you can go for the really big time with an executive jet. The Hawker Siddeley 125's new model, the 800, is the only one actually made in Britain. However, since it travels at nearly 550 m.p.h. with a range of 3500 miles, it is somewhat wasted within the British Isles. Although Miss Wyndham would be delighted to make the cabin the last word in aviation chic, the HS 125 is really excessive for private use, not to mention the expense – nearly £5,000,000 to buy and well over £150,000 per annum to run. Even Frank Sinatra found that he could not afford an earlier model. Given the difficulties of discovering a suitable air-field, you will usually be longer travelling to and from your mini-airliner than actually flying in British airspace.

Whatever form of transport you choose, you are now ready to take off, possibly literally, for the weekend.

# CHAPTER 2

# THE WEEKEND

Nancy Mitford, that satirical but kindly chronicler of the English Upper Classes, wrote of one of her protagonists: 'She filled Hampton every weekend . . . but, although so great is the English predeliction for country life that she generally managed to get these visits extended from Friday to Tuesday, she was left with two empty days in the middle of the week.' The modern hostess may not quite share Lady Montdore's anxieties, but her guests are just as ready to rusticate. These latter day Mr Creeveys, with their delight in 'excellent and plentiful dinners, a fat service of plate, a fat butler, a table with a barrel of oysters and a hot pheasant', are the acme of the English staying in the country. With the advent of the motor car, the country weekend became a mania, depopulated London and its fashionable churches and was strongly deprecated by George V. It still is a mania, as any attempt to leave London on a Friday afternoon will convince you, but you must bear with such inconveniences if you are to participate fully in English social life. You will find that most of your smart weekend invitations centre around some senior sporting event such as a dance, a shoot, a race meeting, a private tennis tournament, or even a Royal visit.

Assuming that there is no specific theme to the weekend, your invitation will come:

a. by letter, giving you a little time to reflect on the prospective delights but not much, since it should be answered by return. Written invitations are the best, as your host will include a map and instructions on how to find the house;

b. by telephone, giving you only a moment's reflection;
c. casually in the bar of the House of Lords, Cheltenham, White's, the Garrick or the women's side of Boodle's which, depending on the time of day, allows even less time to reflect.

Those who live in the country generally have enormous appetites and think nothing of four square meals a day – nursery tea being one of the largest and most important. Whereas before the last war, tea-time was a good moment to arrive, nowadays with fewer staff, even in the grandest of houses, it is likely that your hostess will be busy with a domestic crisis in the kitchen, so do not come before drinks time.

You can arrive:

a. by 'plane – this is considered rather flash unless your house-party is a long way off;
b. by helicopter – considered even flashier unless your host owns one too;
c. by car – when you see it driven off from the front door, do not exclaim that it has been stolen, it is merely the chauffeur (or more likely the garden boy trying it out) parking it at the back of the house. The days when it was polished and filled with petrol from the estate pump are long gone;
d. by train – it may be 'the age of the train' but this civilized practice has largely been spoilt by the vagaries of the British Rail time-table and railway cuts. It is also a bore for your hostess to meet you, and the youngest daughter who has just passed her driving test can be dangerous.

In the grander houses, a list of guests and their allotted bedrooms has been typed out and laid on the hall table; you will be taken to your room by the butler, who may well be Spanish. He carries the cases, unless there is a footman handy. If you have stayed in the house before, the butler will greet you like a long-lost friend. If it is a very grand house with a footman as well, then you dispense what Lady Helen Villiers called a 'footman's nod' – one of recognition without familiarity. Such a peremptory greeting is useful on many other occasions.

As your suitcases will be unpacked for you, make sure that you have used plenty of tissue paper in packing and left out your half bottle of brandy, dirty laundry, unsuitable books and clip-on bow tie. Be equipped with enough warm clothes, the ubiquitous green Hunter wellies (whatever the time of year), tennis racket and plimsolls. It is frowned upon to bring your own croquet mallet or billiard cue.

At around seven o'clock the gong goes for you to change for dinner, but this is usually only a house tradition and the signal to help yourself to another drink. By the time you return to your room, with your drink, your bath will be drawn (run) for you and your clothes laid out on the bed. The grander the house the colder your room, but in exceptional circumstances you will have a coal fire.

Once changed for dinner – Friday nights are generally not smart – you gather back in the drawing room where you meet your fellow guests and a less harrassed hostess before you go into dinner. Since the departure, in Cluedo language, of 'Mrs White the Cook in the Kitchen with the Knife', in most houses the cooking is left to:

a. your hostess – with luck she will be a contributor to *Lady MacLean's Cookbook* and the food will be delicious, certainly better than the boiled nursery fare of the late Mrs White the Cook;

b. your hosts' daughter, who may be a directors' lunch cook, so you will have directors' lunch fare;

c. a cook brought in for the weekend, who will be an awfully nice girl, who was probably at school with your hosts' daughter.

The food, of course, varies as to who cooked it but most country house fare is good and has a strong game flavour about it. The cellar, on the other hand, depends on the vinous knowledge of your host and his forebears.

On Friday night, the after-dinner entertainment is fairly low key, with the late night film on television conscripting most of the guests. The more adventurous continue with conversation, weak whisky and bridge – the more serious punters take to the backgammon board. Watch out for the latter-day version of the thirties' song – 'that bounder your brother who taught you backgammon' – and hope for the intervention of your hostess if you are still losing heavily at four in the morning. You and your fellow guests will drift off to bed when you feel like it, so as to be fit for the next day's entertainment. Before you go to bed, let your hostess know what time you wish to be called and she will tell you the time for breakfast.

Back in your bedroom, you will see that your clothes have been folded up and put away and your bed turned down. In some houses, your host will have copied the Duke of Devonshire who personally selects the books for each of his guest's rooms. Corridor creeping is up to you but first conduct some research into

a. your reception at the other end;
b. your hostess's room, and which of the noisy lap dogs she takes with her to bed.

At the appointed hour the next morning, the 'rusher in' (daily) will bring you tea. Because of the country air, you are ready for breakfast in the dining room, now transformed with a white damask table-cloth. Conversation is limited as guests drift in and tuck into the paper, cereal and, like Saki's Clovis, 'make expeditions among the breakfast dishes' – in the grander houses, they are silver, standing on hot plates. In Scotland, porridge is an essential part of the day; if your host is eating his by the window, do not speak to him until he has finished. It is not obligatory for Sassenachs to eschew sugar on their porridge.

Your hosts will be convinced that their guests are incapable of entertaining themselves, so it is unlikely that you will be left with the morning papers for long, or the good book spotted in the library which you have been longing to read for months. Instead you will be offered, according to season, the choice between

a. tennis – see later;
b. croquet;
c. the first of many long walks interspersed with trips round the garden;
d. a visit to the local antique shops;
e. a visit to another stately open to the public – if you are staying in a house open to the public you will quickly find that you are of more interest to the paying public than any piece of French furniture or Renaissance picture.

Pre-prandial drinks are followed by lunch, usually simple, with nanny and any children who happen to be around. Just as you are settling into the papers again, another form of entertainment is proposed, usually a second walk. In some houses you are expected to work for your fare with a little light gardening until tea. The best teas are to be had in the nursery with nanny, if you think that you can face that and a large dinner. Here nanny is queen and the conversation is directed around her and her charges – usually one of your hosts as well as the children. Several heavy slabs of bread and jam and/or scones, slices of fruit or sponge cake (to be eaten in that order) and lashings of tea later, you stagger down to try to work it off before the next meal.

Dinner on Saturday night is the high point of most weekends. Once again, after the gong you repair for your third bath of the weekend. When you descend, you will meet in the drawing room the neighbours and their house parties who have been invited to dine – one young peer in a Sussex stately home equates one of his dinners with gold plate to ten dinners with his neighbours. The normal rules apply:

a. you talk before dinner to the person next to whom you turn out to be sitting and have run out of conversation by the time that dinner is announced;
b. you are getting on famously when you go into dinner and find that you are at the opposite end of the table to your new friend;
c. you have just found an interesting topic of conversation with your neighbour by the end of dinner, when it is time for the women to leave the dining room.

However, you are all united after dinner for whatever entertainment your hosts have dreamed up. This might entail a foursome of snooker for the men, or some more intellectual game with paper and pencil – the dictionary game, Botticelli (impossible to win if Lord Norwich is in your house party), or the French translation game (consequences are very down beat). Most houses pride themselves on the excellence of their performances of 'the Game' and acting skills come high – usually a hangover from school plays. The more physical go for games such as 'Are You There Moriarty?' In some houses, such as Lord Derby's at Stanley House,

Newmarket, or Knowsley in the north of England, backgammon is still played for huge stakes.

Once again you stagger to bed, only to be woken, seemingly minutes later, with a cup of tea and a call to church. The Catholics go to Mass and a few of the older Church of Englanders make it to Communion. Matins is more of a tradition, with the family pew, plaques and windows. Your host will read the lessons, as his forebears have done for generations, and cough when the sermon has lasted more than twelves minutes (by his hunter).

The vicar is usually asked back for a glass of sherry, visiting prelates stay to lunch. If you have not made it to church, it is the one time when you can catch up on the papers. Every paper

arrives, from the *Sunday Times* and the *Observer* to the *News of the World* and the *People*, and what with the supplements, there is plenty of newsprint to go round. Sunday lunch is traditional roast beef which your host takes pride in carving himself. After lunch, the weekend begins to wind down with the ubiquitous walks and sorties on to the tennis court, ending with tea – outside in summer.

Guests will start to filter away after tea, and you will find that your case has been packed (without your host's book which is what book-plates are for) and placed in your car. When you check your room for the last time, leave a couple of pounds on the dressing table and, depending on the number of staff in the house and the number of your dependents, allow at least £20 for the butler to distribute amongst the rest of the staff. Over-tipping is just as bad as under-tipping. You can give your tip straight to the butler, who will have it out of your hand like a genie as he wishes you a safe journey. Witty remarks about the quality of the weekend are not appreciated in the visitors' book. The grander the house, the less you write that is, name and date only.

Do not be tempted to stay on for dinner, your hosts rarely mean it even if you are invited. Like Lord Home, they 'like having people to stay but when they go, wish they would go'. They have the Sunday film and the repeat of the serial they missed during the week to watch with a tray on their knees in the library.

## COUNTRY HOUSE TENNIS

Tennis, particularly around the Wimbledon Championship fortnight when but *everyone* is at their keenest on court, is an integral part of the weekend and has been so since 1873 when a certain Major Walter Clopton Wingfield invented the game. This Victorian army officer called his invention 'Sphairistike' and first played it on the lawn of his neighbour's house, Nantclwyd, North Wales. If you are a friend of Robin Naylor-Leyland, the present incumbent, he will no doubt show you the exact spot and the plaque. Ever since that august day, tennis, as the Major's game became known by those who could not master the name Sphairistike, has been an essential part of country-house life.

The cry, 'anyone for tennis?', which has thrilled audiences of Womens' Institute plays for decades, equally delights the sportier guests of house parties today. You will find, painfully quickly, that the standards of your hosts and fellow guests differ wildly. They will include:

a. the 'don't play at all's' – generally sincere and should be taken at their word;

b. 'vicarage' – mostly should be classed as 'a';

c. the 'sorry squadron' – infuriating apologies at every missed stroke – generally every stroke;

d. the 'should've brigade' as in 'I should've volleyed' or 'I should've got that in' – equally infuriating as they should've stayed off court;

f. Monsieur Hulot – mostly of the older generation (difficult to shift off court) but generally deadly accurate, standing in long, yellowing flannels in the centre and returning everything seemingly out of reach;

e. country-house – really quite good and keen;

g. good country-house – invariably sickeningly good at everything, including tennis.

In some house parties, tennis is taken very seriously and your invitation can rest on your standards of play. Among the best tennis invitations are:

a. the Marquis of Dufferin and Ava, especially at Clandeboye, Northern Ireland (a good invitation as, even if you do not play tennis, you are guaranteed to meet a most amusing and diverse set);

b. Charlie Lane, half a Rothschild, who plays a healthy game when his mother's pet fox is not sharing the court;

c. Christopher Balfour, a senior player who organizes upmarket tournaments at his home near Henley – good country-house players only;

d. Susie Airde – wins everything.

Dress on the tennis court ranges from the most chic kit from the pages of French *Vogue* at around £200 a time, to whatever you happen to be wearing with the addition of a pair of tatty gym shoes – possibly of the Plimsoll variety. Most houses have an assortment of spare gym shoes and tennis rackets but it is better to take your own in case one, other, or more probably both, are holed. Dress is certainly not an indication of the standard of play.

When a game of tennis is proposed, everyone will hang back, despite the fact that everybody is dying to play. Mens' singles matches are arranged surreptitiously, often for money, by the good country-housers. Mixed doubles are more social and generally of a less high standard. Once on court, you:

a. offer your partner the forehand court and hope he/she does not take it (unless you are sinistral);
b. let your partner serve first, it indicates your confidence in him/her;
c. remember girls' serves or shots are 'only just out', the men's are 'miles away', even if within a millimetre of the line;
d. give the opposition every benefit of every doubt and hope that they do the same to you;
e. regret the extra glass of port after lunch.

Senior tennis house parties happen throughout the year and you may even be asked to sweep the snow off the court – *en tout cas* for players as well as the surface. However, during the winter months, until the end of January, the weekend entertainment is more likely to revolve around your gun.

## SHOOTING

Gamebirds would indeed be flattered if they knew the time, trouble and expense that generations of sportsmen have devoted to shooting them. Although the sporting fraternity does not consider itself to be especially bloodthirsty, it does enjoy shooting as a traditional way of life that has altered little for three hundred years. Such a tradition partly derives from the golden hue with which posterity has painted the eighteenth century ('the squire in his yellow waistcoat in the pheasant-dark woods', wrote Cyril Connolly, that inveterate and lifetime promoter of invitations to the grander house parties), and partly from a memory of enormous Edwardian stands, where the skies were blackened with driven pheasants and the daily toll was in thousands. A lifetime of shooting will have been spent in the company of your trusted friends, the greatest of these being your guns. If they happen to be Purdey's, your descendants will revere your memory the more.

When asked what it was like to possess a pair of Purdey's, one comparatively recent owner replied: 'You remember those cowboy films where the stranger walks into town with pearl-handled pistols? Well, it's like that.' Once you are shooting well with your Purdey's, there is no feeling of exhilaration like it in the world.

However, the road to owning a pair of Purdey's, unless you inherit them, is long and expensive. It can take anything up to three years from start to finish. They can be ordered by mail order (so can super-sabre-jets from the Saks Catalogue), but as in buying a super-sabre-jet, it is better to go personally.

You will find James Purdey and Sons in South Audley Street, established 1814, in the West End of London. They will be expecting you (possibly after breakfast at the Connaught for moral strength) and Sir, and/or Madam will be ushered past wall-to-wall Royal Warrants, interspersed with trophies and photographs of Royal Purdey shooters, their trophies, and of course, their guns, and into the shrine called 'the Long Room'. There, beneath photographs of more Royal Purdey shooters, their guns and their friends, you will be met by the Hon. Richard Beaumont, short and urbane, and as many other of the directors as he can muster (hope for Lord Tryon, tall and genial). Their accountant will also be present, for reasons that will become apparent as the meeting continues.

You will be seated in the interview chair and asked, 'Why do you wish to own a Purdey?' Forewarned is forearmed. Acceptable answers:

    a. they are the best guns in the world and I have dreamed of owning one since my uncle, the Duke, let me touch his when I was twenty-one;
    b. I shoot six days a week here and take partridge shoots in Spain and India, no other gun will stand the pace.

Unacceptable answers:

    a. I wish to have them mounted in perspex and made into a coffee table;
    b. they are a good investment;
    c. I can turn them round at a profit;
    d. my shooting is so lousy, your gats might improve it;
    e. they would go well with my dinky new knickerbocker suit.

Once that august body has decided that you are a fit person to own one, or a pair, of their guns, enter the accountant into the conversation, who will enquire, so discreetly that you hardly notice he is doing it, whether you can afford to pay for the guns at the end of the day (which will be three years hence). The cost should be of secondary importance as the price quoted bears little relation to the final figure, nor does it include the slip (canvas or leather bag for use in the field), travelling case, canvas cover for the travelling case, tools, cleaning kit, gun oil or tow. At the end of the day, allow about £30,000 for the pair, inclusive of extras.

You and your wallet established, you will then be measured for your guns. They will be impressed if you bring your favourite tweed jacket to wear, as you will not be wearing your natty city suiting to shoot. The fitting of your gun, a particular speciality of Purdey's who have been doing it since their foundation, now takes the form of an 'electric' gun with an adjustable stock. On the command, you fire a beam of light at a watercolour of a pheasant on the wall. Boney hands measure where the spot of light falls on the picture to the pheasant's eye and anxious enquiries ensue as to whether 'sir normally wears glasses?'. Your personal preference and your disabilities worked out, you are free to leave.

Many months go by without a word, then, like having a dog in quarantine kennels, reports are sent through on your guns' progress. Unlike having a dog in quarantine kennels, you are forbidden to visit the factory where they are being built by hand. You know you are getting close, or at least closer, to completion, when you hear that 'sir's guns are ready for stocking and would sir like to come in and choose sir's walnut?'. This involves picking two lengths from a pile of rough-hewn French walnut from the Dordogne (not English walnut, but since the Dordogne is now so English anyway, it could be classed as such). Like the doors of your Aston Martin, the stocks of your guns should match, but only X-ray eyes can see the grain. Trust to luck or, sensibly, to Richard Beaumont.

The day comes when it is time to collect your guns, two of seventy made that year. They will be laid out in the Long Room, along with the invoice, equally long. Be enthusiastic but guarded in your comments. Do not be tempted to remark that they are difficult to close (because of the devilish clever mechanism) as that invites the riposte, 'but sir will not be shutting sir's guns anyway, will sir?' In fact, you will soon develop the twisting movement necessary to close them.

Your guns will last all sir's lifetime and the lifetime of your grateful sons and several generations to come. (There are still many Purdey's made in the nineteenth century in use today.) A good second-hand pair will cost not much less than new, but then you do not have your name in Purdey's book, one of 28,000 over nearly two hundred years that include all the greatest shots in the world plus a few rich Texans and Arabs, nor can you send your signed photograph to hang on the wall of the Long Room, beside all the great shots in the world, apart from a few Texans and Arabs. When, like the stranger with the pearl-handled pistols, you shoot everything cleanly that needs to be shot, do not forget to write to your gunsmith to say how the guns are coming along.

The days are long gone when the Prince of Wales (Edward VII) could enquire if a marginally under-dressed friend was 'goin' rattin''. Nowadays shooting clothes, especially in August for grouse, frequently look as if the wearer was going to muck out the stables. That, however, is hardly the point. There is still a correct tenue which, because of its indefinite nature, is even more subtle than the rigidly correct Edwardian dress. Sartorial shooting wear:

    a. a Barbour or thornproof jacket;
    b. stout unpolished boots or Hunter wellingtons;
    c. old leather cartridge case stamped with father's/grandfather's initials;
    d. socks knitted by Aunt Ivy;
    e. anything totally outrageous (hard to beat Lord Glenconner's tartan patchwork shooting suit a.k.a. [affectionately known as] 'the Gathering of the Clans').

Not to wear:

    a. anything new (Lord Home puts stones in the pockets of all new tweed suits to bag them);
    b. anything which matches anything else, especially;
    c. a whistle lanyard that matches the piping of your coat.

# PHEASANTS

Apart from the enjoyment of shooting good, high pheasants, there are other less obvious advantages:

    a. you frequently get a shot at a partridge or a woodcock (for pleasure, King George V equated one partridge to four pheasants, one woodcock to twelve);

    b. for the pot – over-roasted pheasant has always been traditional English autumnal fare – *faisan encore de Norfolk* (you might be luckier to have it stewed in Calvados nowadays, *faisan bon surprise*);

    c. it follows on nicely from shooting grouse and stalking (more later).

There are good places and even better places to shoot pheasant:

    a. Holkham, Norfolk, as the guest of Lord Coke – hope that the Scarborough Clump is shot that day;

    b. Highclere, Hampshire, as guest of the Earl of Carnarvon – only accept if you are a very senior shot as you will meet the highest pheasants in England and the best shots to go with them;

    c. Biddick, Durham, as guest of Lord Lambton – still a good shoot despite his self-imposed exile in Chiantishire;

    d. Stonor, Berkshire, as a guest of Lord Camoys – a good shoot and useful wintertime diversion from the City and Henley Royal Regatta;

    e. Water Priory, Herefordshire, as guest of Sir Robert MacAlpine;

    e. Hambledon, Buckinghamshire, as guest of Lord Hambledon – hope for a good stand at Kings Rise.

There are good shots and there are grand shots and very often you will find that they are one and the same:

    a. The Duke of Marlborough;

    b. Lord Porchester (not called Porchy);

    c. Sir Robert MacAlpine;

    d. Nicholas Cobbold;

    e. Hugh and Geoffrey van Cutsem.

If you are shooting with one of the above, the bag will be considerably increased but do not expect a chance at any of his birds.

There is nothing like a well-run shoot today for a fleeting glimpse into the everyday life of gentle country folk in former, less stringent times. As most shoots have been syndicated, or include paying guns (anyone rich enough between Hawaii and Hobart, the long way round), an invitation to shoot is an expensive present on the part of your host – unless you can ask him back when it counts 'chop for chop'. On accepting the invitation, enquire if it is a double gun day and if you should bring a loader. Forebear to ask if it will be 'a bag or magazine day' (shooting parlance for the number of cartridges you will need – many boxes or just enough to fill your cartridge belt), as the question is rude in that it presupposes there might be little to shoot.

If you have been asked to stay for the weekend (the grander places tend to have their shoots mid-week), arrive in time for dinner the night before. It is a mistake to drink too much or to go to bed too late as it is unfair on:

a. the birds;
b. the butler;
c. your host and hostess;

all of whom, like you, need a clear head the next day. Breakfast is a heady meal, eaten in a state of half dress – stockinged feet and splayed waistcoats. Women, unless shooting (mostly continental), tend to keep to their beds on account of the earliness of the hour and the breakfast noises of the men – grunts, muttered weather prospects, the crackle of *The Times*, and cereals.

Gradually, the hall fills up with

a. other guests;
b. their boots;
c. their clothes;
d. their children and wives brought along to beat, pick up, pass comment, photograph or admire.

Outside the courtyard fills up with

a. Range Rovers;
b. weather-beaten beaters – looking like extras for *Dr Zhivago*;

c.  their dogs, usually scarred terriers, invariably fighting;
d.  gun dogs, too well bred to mingle.

When both camps have assembled, 'hall' meets 'courtyard'. Your host will summon the guns for 'the draw' – not a wild west shootout but a manual ERNIE method of determining the position of the guns, ideally done with numbered, ivory chips in a leather case (the more modern equivalent is dog-eared playing cards or hastily scribbled numbers on a torn up packet of Benson and Hedges). With luck, you will draw a good position for the first drive, and, as you move up two places after each drive, you may strike lucky all day.

On command, you mount the guns' wagon (often like a mobile nissen hut) or clamber into Range or Land Rovers, or big Mercedes 'G' cars. It is a good idea to make friends with:

a.  your loader;
b.  the beaters – they might just head that good high pheasant in your direction;
c.  your neighbours – they may be dangerous or resent you 'wiping their eyes' – not an Optrex operation but success in hitting a difficult bird that they have missed;
d.  your host's dog – undoubtedly his most loved possession.

Once you are established at your stand, practise changing guns with your loader to see that:

a.  he can open sir's Purdey's;
b.  he does not scratch sir's Purdey's (threaten to cut off his buttons if he does);
c.  he can shut sir's Purdey's.

On some shoots, the host and head-keeper are in radio communication, but experience has shown that walkie-talkies invariably pick up messages from air traffic controllers, passing mini-cabs or some pirate radio station, and hosts resort to the horn or a single shot to start each drive. From that first bang or hoot, the day has begun.

Throughout the day, try to avoid:

a.  allowing your dog to chase a fox, herd of deer, your hostess's prize flock of Jacob's sheep – it confuses the pheasants, fox, herd of deer, Jacob's sheep;

b. allowing your dog to savage your birds;
c. allowing your dog to savage your host's birds – a host once asked a guest after his bird had been severely mauled, 'would your dog like a little claret with his pheasant?';
d. allowing your dog to savage your host's dog.

At this point, a Walter Mitty would dream of the pheasants breaking fast and high out of the spinney, the wind behind their tails. He takes the four most difficult birds, swinging through, pivoting on his back foot for the fourth, four dead pheasants in the air at the same time, admiration from the other guns, keepers and beaters. Dream on, but not too long as soon you will hear the cry of 'Over' (not an out of season, vociferous village cricket umpire, but the warning that 'they' are coming over). Once the birds start breaking, shouted instructions follow:

a. 'On the left' – whose left is never made clear, yours or the beaters;
b. 'On the right' – converse direction to your loader's instructions;
c. 'Woodcock' – best shout of all – impressively difficult to shoot and even better to eat.

Your birds are:

a. the ones too high or difficult for your neighbours;
b. the ones within a seemingly much smaller arc than your neighbours;
c. those easier birds poached (not a culinary term) by your neighbours.

With luck, after the first drive, you will have 'your eye in' and your new guns will be behaving properly – this bodes well for the rest of the day and impresses your number one critic, your loader. If you keep missing, he will swear that he can see where the shot went – a grunt is an adequate reply. With luck or good shooting, there is a thick covering of cleanly shot pheasants in front of you (not behind) which should be 'picked' (picked up) by your dog, a keeper or, in practice, your neighbours' dogs. Alternatively, it is better to let your hostess demonstrate the skill of her field-trial champion. Wives/girl-friends, children already bored with beating or a beater's scar-faced terrier are not good substitutes for the field champion in picking your difficult birds.

Back in the mobile nissen hut, you will recognize:

a. the best shots – the ones silent about their performance;
b. the worst shots – the loud ones who match their tweeds;
c. the smell of damp tweed;
d. the smell of damp dog;
e. the smell of anything good in a flask.

Three or four drives later and you are more than ready for the shooting lunch. This takes the form either of a picnic, brought by you on less grand shoots and eaten behind a haystack, or a more sophisticated sit-down lunch. For the former, guard against bringing anything too exotic, you have only a one in ten chance of eating it yourself. Proper lunch is eaten either in a tenant's kitchen – vacated by him for the day like the Highland Clearances, the shooting-lunch room at home, or possibly the dining room. The grander the shoot, the hotter the lunch and the less there is to drink – save for the obligatory glass of port afterwards.

On again after lunch for another three or four drives until it is dark. You know it is dark as you see:

a. the flashes out of your barrels;
b. pheasants as silhouettes;
c. owls and bats;
d. your loader yawn.

Before you repair to the shooting tea – and you are ready for it despite that hearty breakfast and hot lunch – there is the signing-off ceremony. The bag is laid out and counted (with luck the headless or mangled pheasants are not yours). Your loader gives you your personal tally and you give him his tip. The head-keeper has a brace of pheasants put in the boot of your car and, in one fluid movement of touching his hat with the index finger of the left hand, shakes your hand with the right, removing the five pound notes you have expertly stuck to your palm with a quick lick.

Over tea the day is relived, drive by drive, and the performance of the better guns discussed. Before you leave, you will be given a shooting card with the name of the other guns, the weather and the bag. On grand shoots, this is sent later on a post card. Either way, the information and your comments should be transferred to your game-book as soon as possible. The really good shots write in black ink with their tally of woodcock in red.

At the end of the day you hope that:

a  you shot well enough to be asked back;
b. you impressed your neighbour enough for him to ask you to shoot with him/her;
c. one day you will shoot like the aged, myopic colonel who accounted for fifty per cent of the bag.

## GROUSE

Once you have mastered the vagaries of shooting pheasants, you can graduate to grouse. If you thought that you were an adequate shot, you are in for a shock when you arrive on the moor, for grouse are a new shooting experience. They have the edge over pheasants as:

a. the red grouse (lacopagus Scoticus Scoticus) is only found in the British Isles so foreigners have to come to us if they wish to shoot it. One Greek shipping millionaire did try to introduce them on his Saronic Islet but they tired of Greek food and retsina and soon died;
b. they have a strong sense of self-preservation and fly with that in mind. Seemingly closely related to the Spitfire, they manoeuvre as such. To ground them needs steel for nerve and determination and lead, No. 6 shot, from your cartridges;
c. they are extremely good to eat – roasted or possibly in a pie. Turn a deaf ear to your expensive cook's entreaties to do anything else.

Shooting grouse is becoming more exclusive as annually there are fewer and fewer grouse to shoot. They are susceptible to everything:

a. good shots;
b. ticks;

c. every disease save herpes – at the time of writing;

d. sheep;

e. the Forestry Commission;

g. water – either too much (drowns the chicks) or too little (die of thirst).

Thus the days when a moor was valued at £2000 per pair of breeding grouse, regardless of acreage, are long over. Scotland, suffering from too much rain, the Forestry Commission and ticks, is losing her grouse moors rapidly. However, to guarantee a good day's grouse shooting try:

a. Bolton Abbey, Yorkshire, as guest of the Duke and Duchess of Devonshire;

b. Cortachy Castle, Angus, Scotland, as guest of Lord Airlie – a jolly, mixed party that can include Stan, their London milkman, on his Scottish sojourn;

c. Leadhills, Lanarkshire, as guest of the Marquess of Linlithgow;

d. Canda Craig, Aberdeenshire, as guest of Faulkner Wallace, good moor but hope for invitation before it is finally sold;

e. Invercauld, Aberdeenshire, as guest of Alwyne Farquarson – Britain's largest landowner (290,000 acres) within a ring fence. Do not show surprise at the low butts – the laird caters for syndicates from the Orient. The obvious jokes about the piper at dinner doubling as the estate plumber are wearing thin;

d. Stainly, Yorkshire, as guest of Lord Mountgarrett – the hot-air balloons fly better than his grouse.

You can either 'walk up' or shoot driven grouse. For walking up you need to be extremely fit and have a kind host to give you the day's shooting. To shoot driven grouse you do not have to be quite so fit but need an even kinder host. Shooting grouse is basically similar to shooting pheasants, save that:

a. it is generally warmer (August onwards);

b. you hide behind a butt – these can be quite cosy affairs built of stone with a heather-thatched top;

c. beaters are often convicts or Borstal boys (soldiers at Balmoral) – no broad arrows but they come complete with their warders.

Accidents are not infrequent on the grouse moor. Your neighbours (and you) will be relieved to see:

a. sticks on top of the butt to stop you swinging too far;
b. no sign or sound of your dog;
d. no sign of your wife/husband/lover unless as a free loader;
e. no one about to emulate a certain baronet who shot his father and was thereafter known as 'Baghdad'.

Another advantage of shooting grouse is that, because of the remoteness of most moors, especially in Scotland, you have to be asked to stay, which means that you will undoubtedly be party to other diversions, inside and out of doors. One such diversion in Scotland could be a day 'on the hill'.

## STALKING

To those who have never stalked, the description of a 'day on the hill' sounds like a foretaste of hell; to those who have stalked, there is nothing like it for exhilaration and satisfaction (in retrospect). It is physically so demanding that only those who underwent a public school education or SAS training could dare to say they enjoyed it.

You can only stalk in the wilder and more inaccessible parts of Scotland, and the problems of moving about the country make it a difficult and exclusive sport. It is, of course, better to be invited, but, failing that, you can rent a week's stalking for around £1200, with the hire of lodge, food, drink, cook, tips and any fishing on the go for at least another £1000 – the single haunch of venison you are allowed to take home at the end of the week is free. Among the best, and grandest, places to stalk are:

a. Balmoral   plenty of room for family and friends;
b. Kinveachy Forest – home of the Earl of Seafield   90,000 acres, enough room for most stags;
c. Blair Atholl – the home of the Duke of that name;
d. Kinlochewe – the Whitbread stalking estate – hope you are

taken to the north end. Anything within ten miles of the lodge is kept for German lager makers etc.

Before you take to 'the hill', you need a .270 or .275 rifle from any of the leading gunsmiths such as Rigby, Purdey or Holland and Holland, and this will cost you in excess of £3000. Today it is not frowned on to use a telescopic sight. If you are lucky enough to have the right introduction, David Lloyd will build you an 'all in one' version with the telescope incorporated into the rifle. You can always borrow a rifle from your host but it is better to have your own – at least you can damn your own rifle for a bad shot. You will also need a stalking Thesaurus in order not to be totally misled. For:

a. deer forest, read approximately 20,000 acres of bare Scottish heather, peat bog and water with six trees in the bottom right hand corner;
b. hill, read a 3000 foot mountain, over 3000 feet is a 'Munro';
c. mist, read rain;
d. mist, read impenetrable fog;
e. mist, read blinding thunderstorm – none of the above any excuse to stay at home;
f. a Royal or twelve pointer, read stags which you would like to shoot (looks good mounted on the wall) but which your host or stalker has inevitably reserved for someone other than you;
g. a hummel, a switch, a stag going back, read animals you would not dream of mounting (no horn, one horn or bad horns), but which your stalker insists you shoot and your host would like shot.

As will become increasingly obvious as you get into stalking, there are certain taboos:

a. carrying binoculars instead of a telescope;
b. complaining about mist, hail, boulders, bounders, midges, cramp, thirst, or indeed, anything at all;
c. shooting at anything that your stalker has not grudgingly approved or for that matter not approved;
d. missing anything that your stalker has grudgingly approved;

e. wounding anything that your stalker has grudgingly approved.

That live-long moment when you actually squeeze the trigger of your rifle and your stag falls is an infinitesimal part of the sport, for there is much torture before that moment and more, much more, after. The day starts not too early with a good breakfast (which you will soon regret) after which you will meet your stalker. He, like you, will be dressed in tweeds, but there the resemblance ends. He will expect to carry your rifle but will think highly of you if you carry it yourself. He will not notice the weight, merely your attitude as you hand it over. You may walk to the home beat but more often you are driven miles in an ancient jeep or Land Rover on unrecognizable roads (or go by boat) to the farthest point of the estate. If very unlucky, you walk the unrecognizable roads to the farthest point of the estate.

Before you can begin to stalk, you need to be at the top of the hill. As you climb, all you will see through sweaty eyes, is:

a. the short stubby legs (like milk bottles) of your stalker relent-
lessly pounding the heather, at the same pace regardless of
gradient;
b. heather that seemingly grows taller and thicker the higher
you climb;
c. crows and ravens (with luck looping the loop);
d. a vision of a rest before you reach the top.

When that blessed rest finally comes, you curse that you have
brought so many clothes. However, this is the only time you will
be warm (in fact boiling) all day for, from the time the stalk begins
to the time you return to your bath, you will be cold, wet, cross,
dirty, seized in every muscle and bitten mercilessly on all exposed
flesh – not necessarily in that order, but certainly suffering from
them all before the day is out.

After the shortest of rests, your stalker will bring out his telescope to look for your stag. With a grunt, he will show you the
one that you will stalk, which, despite the telescope, looks more
like a boulder in the heather. What you do recognize, however,
is that it is a very, very long way off across decidedly hostile
country. Your progress will be prone, painfully slow and slowly
painful. You will slither through peat bogs, sheep droppings,
slimy mud and running streams, your eyes fixed firmly on the
seat of your stalker's plus fours as you crawl in his wake. After
what seems like many hours, and probably is, you will have been
led into a position to shoot your stag. Your stag will be the one
which is:

a. sitting down;
b. behind a better one that is not your stag;
c. behind a wild goat or woolly sheep;
d. the wrong end on.

In these cases, all you can do is wait for your stag to present
itself properly so that you can shoot it cleanly through the neck –
making noises like another stag, grating a stone or tapping your
stick can be dangerous as that could be the end of the stalk. While
waiting, you can at least catch your breath and take in something
other than your stalker's plus fours – the magic of the moor, its
remoteness, the soaring birds and the silence. Eventually, you

will have your shot, usually only one, so it has to be the *coup de grâce*.

The stag dead and the echo of the crack of your rifle still in your ears, your stalker will be off, knife in hand, for the gralloch. This operation of disembowelling the stag is not for the squeamish. Try not to recall your breakfast as the stalker sticks his knife into the beast to slit open the stomach, then plunges his arms (up to his biceps) into the beast to draw out the entrails. Up to this point, only a third of the way through the day, your stag is thought of as the 'noble beast' but from now on, it is the 'bloody beast' (or a great deal worse) as you start your homeward journey. Stags are invariably dropped in inaccessible places and have to be dragged to where they can be picked up by the scruffy and ancient pony with an even more ancient pony boy or, by the modern variant, a motorised Argocat (an eight-wheeled machine that makes a dreadful noise and rarely works in the hands of the ancient pony boy). Getting your stag to the pony boy involves:

  a. dragging it very slowly up the sheer face of the hill;
  b. it dragging you and the stalker very fast down the sheer face of the hill.

On the ascent, your stag takes its revenge by applying its natural brakes, the points of its horns, in the heather, and appears heavier by the yard – these brakes, however, do not act when you are hurtling downhill. Your wife/girl-friend, who has been foolish enough to accompany you, will have the task of carrying your rifle, telescope, coat, waistcoat, lunch box and anything else you were stupid enough to bring that morning, except your stick which has been tied to the antlers to prevent them snapping off. By now you hate:

  a. your wife/girl-friend – the 'I'm not going to the Oban Ball with rope burns on my shoulder for the third year running' wears thin;
  b. the stalker – the 'come on now, sir, only a wee bit further' wears thin;
  c. the pony boy;
  d. the bloody beast;
  e. stalking.

When you arrive at the point where you can be reached by the pony boy, he will not be there as:

a. he has forgotten which button to press to switch on his walkie-talkie;
b. he is asleep;
c. he cannot start the Argocat;
d. he cannot find his pony.

Eventually, the pony boy does arrive and your stag is bundled on to the bonnet of the jeep and driven furiously back to the granite lodge (*anglicé* large mansion with twenty bedrooms with baths to match) where you are staying. There, with tea and whisky and the only admiring glance from your wife/girl-friend that you can count on all day, your stag is ritually weighed. The details will be entered into the stag book and the carcass tagged and sent to Germany via a game merchant. After your bath and another glass of whisky you are almost human again. Then, and only then, is your faith restored in the joys of stalking. Once again, you can relive those experiences 'on the hill' that never fail to remind you that God was a Stuart on His Mother's side.

## THE SCOTTISH WEEKEND

Apart from the pleasures to be had 'on the hill', or in the rivers, there are many other diversions for the hedonist in the Scottish season. For the energetic and the hearty, there are the eight highland balls – from the Oban Ball to the Perth Hunt Ball, you can criss-cross the Highlands, staying in draughty castles, and dance the night away until breakfast with wild reels and weak whisky.

Less strenuous are the house parties around the Borders in August, where the hills are more genteel and the pace more gentle. The houses are no less striking, many being Glasgow industrialists' Victorian copies of Scottish Baronial – light grey or red sandstone, embellished with all the right features of a grand Scottish seat – turrets, turrets on turrets, and castellations. Inside the hall, past the rows of boots, mackintoshes and fishing rods, you are met by acres of tartan carpet, purple and light green a favourite, solid Victorian furniture and your hosts – in that order.

You will find that your fellow guests have come from the pages of:

a. the Court Circular – Princess Margaret and most of her ladies-in-waiting are Border-Scotia-habitués after the Balmoral sojourn;
b. Variety – the stars of stage and screen from both sides of the Atlantic;
c. Hansard – from both Chambers;
d. Interiors – interior decorators and their clients;
e. the more up-market gossip columns – from a. to d. above.

Your stay is basically like any traditional weekend in the country, only almost everything, regardless of the weather (cf page 00), takes place outside. At that time of the year it should be hot and dry, but you can never be certain of anything in Scotland.

Extra-mural entertainment:

a. picnic lunches in the heather by the loch – whisky and midges an essential element;
b. lunch by the swimming pool – at Glen, the seat of The Master of Mustique, a half-lifesize white marble statue of Roy Roy scowls at the mist rising off the water heated to 80°F;
c. a walk over the estate – nothing increases the self-righteousness so much as a stiff walk, particularly in the rain;
d. roller-skating – bring your own skates;
e. photographic sessions – do not forget to photograph your hostess in your eagerness to be included in every other group.

Away-day entertainment:

a. visit to the Palace of Holyroodhouse – tour leader, HRH the Princess Margaret;
b. visit to the Edinburgh Festival – best seats guaranteed;
c. visit to Traquair House, the oldest inhabited house in Scotland. It is likely that the laird, Peter Maxwell-Stuart, will show you round – he will certainly sell you some frightfully strong beer brewed by himself;
d. visit to the local knitwear factories, where you can stock up on all those sweaters you could never afford at home.

Intra-mural activities:

   a. talking;
   b. games – paper, pencil and dictionary providend; any time of
      the day or night, mostly old music hall songs (piano, HRH
      the Princess Margaret if staying);
   c. singing;
   d. amateur theatricals.

The party over and you join the great exodus south and the
start of the London season. On leaving – do not be tempted to
sign the visitors' book on the same page as HRH, you will not be
able to rub your signature out later.


## THE POP WEEKEND

So much for the traditional house party that you will find in
varying forms of grandeur throughout Britain and throughout the
year. It has always been a feature of the British aristocracy that
they have been prepared to recruit into their ranks those whom
they found amusing from whatever background. Today, the jockeys, prize fighters, and chorus girls of Regency romances have
been replaced by racing drivers and film and rock stars from both
sides of the Atlantic. However, if the Hon. David and Chryssie
Lytton-Cobbold were to invite you to stay at Knebworth House
in Hertfordshire for the first weekend in July, your fellow guests
(the members of a major rock group or famous jazz band) would
be there to entertain not you, but the 100,000 others camped in
the park.

The British aristocracy are survivors and not above selling any
part of themselves to continue in the manor/manner of their
forefathers. Many marry American heiresses, indeed any heiress
would do in a financial crisis. Other landowners sent their tenants
below ground to mine coal, while the present generation lure the
sons and daughters of those same tenants back to their parks
above ground for all forms of entertainment. Like many of the
women in the Lytton family since the fifteenth century, Chryssie
Cobbold works overtime to keep the roof on the house, hence the
annual pop festival (the house, interior and life-style are more

recognizable from the film *The Shooting Party* than the bad horror films on late night television).

To experience the full flavour of the pop or jazz festival at Knebworth, it is wise to turn up a day or two early (there is a landing platform at the end of the drive if you come by helicopter). You might then also witness such scenes as the legendary conflict when the final sing-song of the local Girl Guides' camp overlapped with the dress rehearsal of the Rolling Stones' performance. Anyone who has known a Brown Owl will know whose music floated out over the park. You will also witness the transformation of a pleasant English country house park into a scene reminiscent of a grand tiger hunt – a jungle of scaffolding poles, a sea of tents and tens of thousands of people. The central tent is known as the 'crash-out' where the tentless stay – unless a keen voyeur, forbear to put your head in after lights out.

The day, always a Saturday, starts early for everyone. After breakfast in the kitchen, you will be sent down before the gates open (six o'clock) to stake out the Cobbold corral with sleeping bags, children and proprietorial stares (no elbows for, unlike football crowds, your fellow fans are a peaceful lot).

Pop *sine qua non* (the new Lytton-Cobbold motto):

a. a flag on a long bamboo, essential to mark your position in the multitude so that you can find your way to and from your patch – do not be tempted to take an armorial flag from the hall nor to have one commissioned by the Queen Mary's School of Needlework, try asking Marc or some similar cartoonist to design yours or make it up yourself;

b. contents of the games cupboard – Scrabble, cards, bridge markers;

c. all the newspapers, from the *Financial Times* to the *New Musical Express*;

d. food in large wicker hampers – it is going to be a long day and there are many to cater for;

e. not much to drink – as you will soon be surrounded by thousands of people, it is difficult to go to one of the many lavatories and even harder to find your way back.

You will, all too quickly, discover that it is unwise to:

a. let your neighbours know where you are staying, particularly in a county voice;
b. wear anything but jeans – preferably with badges – as otherwise it will be you who stands out against the amazing polychrome punks;
c. comment on the herbal cigarettes of your neighbours and their unusual smell; if offered one, give it back after a couple of puffs;
d. ask for Coca Cola as coke – if given something that resembles talcum powder, do not sprinkle it on your body;
e. bring a Barbour or umbrella – the heat from such a multitude is enough to discourage any potential rain-cloud;
f. eat at the Hari Krishna free food tent – you could easily experience Siva's Revenge.

The concert starts at midday with a succession of minor groups. Being so near the stage, you can at least see the performers but, as they are surrounded by mountains of speakers, the noise is unbelievable. Refuge behind a Sony Walkman and earphones playing Mozart sonatas is not what this concert is about. The main group do not appear until after ten o'clock. In the seventies, they had such stars as the Rolling Stones, Pink Floyd, Genesis, Led Zepplin and the Boom Town Rats, but now it is more of a jazz festival.

After the concert has finished, around midnight, there is a party in the long gallery and drawing room of the house for the chosen few, where you will meet the group and their hangers-on. The security guards and police, including the drug squad, also come in for a drink; liggers – the group's groupies – are kept out. The party goes on until dawn when the house party liggers crash out and the group go off in their helicopters.

As the park slowly depopulates, including the several babies born there each year and many more conceived, you will pick your way through acres of rubbish as you too take your leave. It may not have been a typical weekend in the country but at least it was, in its own peculiar way, the Very Best of British.

# CHAPTER 3

# THE ARTS

There are few places where the pursuit of the Very Best of British is so well demonstrated as in the Arts. Those august bodies, made up of experts, politicians, philanthropists, retired civil servants and other useful members of society, who administer the Arts, try to recreate Parnassus (complete with all the Muses) in London and the provinces. Whether they succeed or not is a matter of opinion, but, undeniably, they do their best.

## GLYNDEBOURNE

Although the eccentric idea of transporting opera, that most urban of art forms, to the country is not uniquely British (the Italians do it at Torre del Lago for Puccini, the French at Avignon), only in Britain could you find a fully equipped, 800-seat opera house virtually inaccessible to all recognized forms of transport. Only the British, regardless of the vagaries of their weather, would dress up in black tie and long dresses shortly after lunch so as to picnic in the garden and fill every seat of that opera house for sixty-six performances each year, with tens of thousands of disappointed operaphiles hard on their heels. The scene is the Glyndebourne Festival Opera; the place is near Lewes in Sussex, fifty miles south of London; the patrons are diverse, and the eccentric Englishman who began it all was the late John Christie.

Christie had previously been a science master at Eton (the headmaster once found his butler dispensing coffee to his class while he finished his bath), before he inherited his considerable estates. Once rusticated, the keen music lover set about putting culture into agriculture. He started by adding the Organ Room to the East wing, the site of an Eton Fives court, then began work on an organ to encourage his Eton friend and mentor, Dr Charles Lloyd, to visit him. Unfortunately his friend died, so the organ was never finished, although the room was used for amateur productions. Later, a young soprano, Audrey Mildmay, was engaged to raise the standard of an otherwise amateur operatic performance and, much to everyone's surprise, Christie married her. With his talented wife, his ambition grew and in the early thirties, he decided to build a small theatre. Mrs Christie told him firmly: 'If you're going to spend all that money, John, for God's sake do the thing properly.' He took his wife's advice and, largely with the estate labour, built a three hundred seat theatre to present opera in 'an undisturbed atmosphere'. The Glyndebourne Festival Opera opened in 1934 with two Mozart operas, *Le Nozze di Figaro* followed by *Cosi fan tutti*, and, apart from the War years, it has continued to float Mozart, as well as many other composers, out over the Sussex Downs.

Patrons can be divided into:

a. operaphiles who know a good production when they see one – distinguished by faded dinner jackets for the men, flat heels for the women (against sodden lawns and mud), and heavy coats for both. Picnic: hamper with non-vintage champagne or Chablis, anything gamey. Comment: enlightened criticism;

b. the 'hurry-up-or-we-will-be-late-for-the-interval' brigade, mostly from the financial world impressing clients – distinguishable by mackintoshes over dinner jackets and women in high heels. Picnic: vintage champagne in styrofoam ice chests, Scottish smoked salmon or similar out of plastic picnic box. Comment: undiscerning praise;

c. the *eleganti*, the internationally rich who attend in style, well-dressed. Picnic: served by butler and eaten in comfort with table and chairs, damask table cloths, candelabra, crystal and silver. Comment: comparisons with La Scala, Milan and the New York Met;

d. the *cognoscenti*, those within the opera world or heavy supporters of it, who would not dream of picnicking but dine in the house with the present director, Sir George Christie, his wife, Mary and pug, Smutty. Comment: Thank you for dinner.

Much of the charm of Glyndebourne is the setting – the Sussex Downs that roll, the mature trees that lend grandeur, and the water (in the form of three ponds – not lakes, 'lakes are what you have up north' said Christie Senior) that is essential to every gentleman's residence. Within this setting are beautiful gardens and wide lawns that are at your disposal, weather permitting. Everything, of course, depends on the weather.

Having overcome the Herculean task of obtaining tickets, you set out for Glyndebourne. You can arrive:

a. by train – from Victoria. The sight of you in your dinner jacket or long dress in the early afternoon now arouses curiosity only among the tourists;
b. by car – if you bring your chauffeur, he can join a chauffeur's convention in an outhouse during the performance;
c. by helicopter – do not forget to clear it first before you plonk down.

It is best to arrive in time to stake out your picnic spot. Anywhere but the car park is good. Try the Wild Garden, the semi-circular lawn beside the Audrey Mildmay Memorial Garden, or the Ha-Ha Lawn in front of the main terrace. The ponds are good for cooling bottles but beware of the mosquitoes (if you fall in retrieving your bottle, you may be kitted out from the wardrobe department with a suit from the Bal Blanc from the final act of *Eugene Onegin*). After tea, wander round the gardens. You do not have to be a latter-day Paxton or Vita Sackville-West to appreciate the various periods of English garden and the way they blend with each other and the setting. You will stroll through Tudor gardens with high yew hedges (the Urn Garden), or formal walled gardens, along terraces bursting with flowers and climbing plants, past eighteenth century vistas of parkland and well-stocked herbaceous beds. You can take in the three ponds and the visiting fauna on the second pond's Duck Island, even cross the ha-ha to The Vinegars or behind to Lawn Hill. Resist remarking on how the sheep look as

if they were on wires and had been painted by Oliver Messell or how the Friesian cattle resemble your male fellow promenaders in dinner jackets – one very short-sighted academic remarked: 'How marvellous that the orchestra plays cricket in the interval.'

The tempo moves up. Division bells sound like a fire alarm, with luck the only discordant note you will hear all evening. It is essential not to be late for the performance as *nothing* interrupts that (even the announcement of John Christie's death was kept to the end of *Cosi fan tutti*). If you are late, you can at least watch a televised version in the Organ Room until there is a suitable pause in the opera. Unless you are a guest of the Christies or someone pretty senior on the staff, you will be in the auditorium where you will have a good view wherever you sit – beware of the four resident bats that time their entrance to coincide with the final act.

Glyndebourne seems to please everyone, whatever their reason for being there; the description 'Eden on a day return' is not far wide of the mark. For those hours you live in an illusory world. Glyndebourne is undeniably an anachronism, but it is an anachronism that works.

## COVENT GARDEN

Every year, there is a handsome cake by way of a grant of cash voted by the Government to the Arts. Its size and richness vary greatly according to which party happens to be in power, but what is constant is that the largest slice, known as the Taglioni cake, is always gobbled up by the Royal Opera House, Covent Garden.

At Covent Garden, the Royal Opera and the Royal Ballet cohabit amicably, sharing the stage and orchestra during the year and alternating their performances – a nightmare for scene-shifters and lighting crews but lovely for you if you enjoy both opera and ballet. You will attend the performance staged by the Royal Ballet as:

   a. you have been an *aficionado* since you saw Moira Shearer in *The Red Shoes* and are so keen that you do not mind if you have to stand at the back of the amphitheatre;

   b. you have been invited by your stockbroker, dentist, department store, gas man or grocer as their guest in the stalls;

   c. you have been invited by one of the Board of Directors, from the Chairman, Sir Claus Moser to the General Director, Sir

John Tooley, and so take the Royal Box if it is free, the Bedford Box if not;

d. you have been asked by Sir Kenneth MacMillan, or the grand old man of ballet, Sir Frederick Ashton, to join them in the centre front of the Grand Tier to comment on their choreography;

e. you are a guest of a member of the Royal Family, the grandest invitation of all.

If yours is a royal invitation, then you will arrive with the Royal party at their own side entrance in Floral Street. You will shed your coats in the King's Smoking Room, a replica of Edward VII's cabin on the Royal Yacht *Victoria and Albert*. (Note the door ahead which now leads to the royal lavatory. This originally gave on to a handy staircase up to the side of the stage to facilitate quick entry and exit for members of the chorus.) As you go up the stairs, pause to take in Edward VII's lemon squeezer and David Hockney's portrait of a past General Administrator, Sir David Webster. Through the double doors at the top of the stairs you will enter the ante-room with its splendid domed, plaster ceiling, carved fireplace (with electric bars and logs) and table laid for dinner. If you are attending a Gala Performance, then you will go through to the Royal Box with the house lights blazing and the audience rising to their feet (all save ballet-loving republicans). If it is an ordinary performance, then all that will be seen in the auditorium is a pencil of light as the royal party slip into their seats.

The Royal Box, like the rest of the Opera House, is gold, red and plush. Your hosts will bag the best seats, more like thrones, in gilt and red velvet with a royal cypher at the top, while you make do with a less grand, but still comfortable, arm-less chair. If you are a second-rate guest then you will only make the sofas and will have to watch the performance by way of a looking glass on the wall angled somewhere towards the centre of the stage. However, that is only marginally less satisfactory than the in-adequate view from the front row of the Royal Box – Princess Margaret, who knows a thing or two about ballet and the Royal Opera House, always sits in the centre of the Grand Tier for the best view in the House. When in the Royal Box, forebear to:

a. lean forward and rest your arms on the balcony in front of your host;
b. squint through your opera glasses, searching for your friends in the stalls;
c. drop your programme on ballet-loving republicans below;
d. show surprise at the continual movement of the orchestra – the smaller fry are constantly nipping out for a swift glass of beer during the performance;
e. comment adversely on the third level of candelabra – a present from the Queen Mother to the Royal Opera House.

Although you have a lousy view from the Royal Box, you are at least spared having to fight your way to and around the aptly-named Crush Bar for your drink during the intervals (the experts order their champagne and smoked salmon sandwiches before the performance). Instead you saunter back to the ante-room for a quick and civilized dinner. The fare ranges from a cold buffet to a full-scale up-market, take-away dinner sent over from the nearby l'Interlude de Cabaillou.

Your conversation will revolve round the performance, and you will hear informed snippets like:

a. did you notice at the end of Wayne's solo the un-choreographed two finger movement directed towards the conductor after he dragged his tempo?;
b. Dame Ninette de Valois (Madame) must be in the House – the *corps* (the young lovelies) looked terrified;
c. how brave of Lynn Seymour to bare *all* in her autobiography.

To be invited backstage to a dressing room after the performance is not as exciting as it should be (the opera stars fare better in the new wing). The dressing rooms are scruffy, and noisy too as the sounds of the scene shifters and orchestra packing up are relayed by intercom to the dressing rooms backstage. Far better that the stars should come to you for a glass of champagne in the ante-room of the Royal Box before you swirl away in the Royal 'limmo' from your private entrance.

Whatever the ballet, it will still only be about half past ten when you leave. If in a Royal party, it is likely that you will be asked back for a night cap and scrambled egg on crisp fried bread at

Kensington Palace (KP) – Maids of Honour House in Princess Court for Princess Margaret, Apartments 8 and 9 for the Prince and Princess of Wales or Clock Court for Prince and Princess Michael of Kent. If you are in the Queen Mother's party then you will return to Clarence House (The Clarence) where you are in for a very late night.

If yours is a non-Royal party, you will have to make do with the tail end of someone else's dinner party or slip into Annabels.

## DINNER AND A VISIT TO THE VICTORIA AND ALBERT MUSEUM WITH DR SIR ROY STRONG

'The museum,' G. K. Chesterton wrote, doubtless with the Victoria and Albert in mind, 'is not meant either for the wanderer to see by accident or for the pilgrim to see with awe. It is meant for the mere slave of a routine of self-education to stuff himself with every sort of incongruous intellectual food in one indigestible meal.' The art that the British were not good at creating themselves, they bought or looted from foreigners. From pictures of the Medici to the Elgin Marbles, from the furniture of Versailles to the Ashanti gold, the great treasures of the world were crated up and shipped home, first to the Palladian mansions and later to the Victorian museums. It can not be said that the majority of Englishmen were grateful – they were indifferent to the collecting activities of Charles I and never forgave the Prince Regent for having taste – but the result is a wealth of alien objects in British museums that is only just beginning to be rivalled by the Americans.

If you are grand enough, or rich enough and remotely interested in the Arts (with a capital A), it is not unlikely that you will be invited to dine with the present director of the Victoria and Albert Museum, Dr Sir Roy Strong and Lady Strong. She is only a keeper's daughter and better known to herself as Miss Julia Trevelyan Oman. Roy, who would have liked to have put the roy in royal but only got as far as Croydon, took over the museum in 1974 from John-if-I-say-it-is-a-Cellini-then-it-is-a-Cellini-Pope-Hennessy when the Government granted an export licence for 'the Pope' to go to America.

The venues for intimate feasts within the museum are endless, but a favourite place for the good doctor to entertain is in the music room rescued from the late Norfolk House and furnished with contemporary furniture from other parts of the museum. You might be even luckier and dine at No. 1 London, Apsley

House, home of the Duke of Wellington, or Ham House, both of which are colonies of the V and A.

The director usually gives his dinners to go with a sneak preview (or the opening) of a major exhibition, so your fellow guests are chosen with the exhibition in mind. The guest list is made up of those who have lent to the exhibition, royal, ducal (any number to choose from) or foreign; academics and the intelligentsia; a smattering of art politicians, Paul and Ingrid Channon, Grey Gowrie or Norman St John Stevas; an actor or two such as Donald Sinden. Even dress designers, Jean Muir and Zandra Rhodes, are asked. Members of the V and A staff also attend – not too many 'otherwise it is like a works outing'.

Whoever you are, you are searched at the entrance before being allowed into the gallery where you will meet your fellow guests and the director, who will be standing like Hilliard's 'Young Man Among the Roses'. At a given signal, extraneous guests will be ushered out, leaving the rest of the field, about sixty of you, clear for dinner upstairs. The white and gold Norfolk House Music Room will be beautiful with cream flowers, white candles in some of the museum's candelabras, and silver specially commissioned for such dinners. The *place-à table* (leave *placement* to ladies' maids applying for a position) is done by Sir Roy himself – some tables, like Marcus Binney's, are better than others for conversation. The food and wine are always excellent, except that your host insists on cheese and salad (green salad only so as not to upset the colour scheme). At the end of dinner, Dr Sir Roy will rise to his feet with his eyes firmly on the ceiling and make a flummery speech. Do not be tempted to smoke (unless you are Princess Margaret) as the resident fireman will put it out for you – if you want a crafty cigarette, join the smokers pacing up and down the Cromwell Road.

Dinner over, you can either go back to the exhibition or accept an invitation from Dr Sir Roy Strong Ph.D., FSA to tour 'his' museum.

While the doctor is pointing out:

a. how well the Department of the Environment have cleaned the entrance hall and the new shop;
b. the colour of the D. of E. paint, British Standard Colours only;

c. the phoni Soni [sic] television camera;

d. the floor mosaics laid in the 1890s by female convicts, *opus criminale*, and recently uncovered;

e. the vistas he is creating through the galleries – at the expense of the objects;

f. the antiques (like eighteenth-century Italian sculpture) with which he 'decorates' the galleries;

it is essential not to miss the really fine pieces of the museum – for this take a sneak reading of the authoritative work, *The Victoria and Albert Museum* by Anna-should-I-compare-thee-to-a-Somers Cocks.

It is unwise to ask why:

a. there are no exhibitions at the V and A other than gold, sex or death;

b. the Knight of Glyn made the new Regency Gallery resemble a duty free shop;

c. the buttocks of Canova's 'Sleeping Nymph' appear to be overcleaned;

d. a couple went into the base of Trojan's Column with more than a hint of Tiberian glint in their eyes;

e. the fakes gallery is the fastest expanding gallery in the museum.

Where you can never be absolutely sure that any piece in the museum is absolutely 'right', the one gallery where everything is 100% genuine is the fake's corridor that now houses some of the former finest, and most expensive pieces, in the museum. Notwithstanding this, in the words of that fine, fat Frenchman in his pneumatic suiting, 'the Victoria and Albert Museum is certainly worth a detour'.

# CHAPTER 4

# THE HORSE

While marketing companies divide up their consumers by number and letter, and sociologists their subjects into ethnic, religious and class groups, the British upper classes have a simpler and more effective method. Britain is composed of those who ride and care about horses and those who do not. For the former, the horse occupies most of their waking moments, not to say a good deal of their money as well. There are plenty of equine options open to them for the horse is a versatile animal. Depending on the time of year, the type of horse and your hippocratic preference, you can hunt, jump fences, race, race and jump fences at the same time, or play polo from their backs. When age and/or shortage of funds (horses are very expensive whatever their provenance) force you out of active participation, you can still gain considerable pleasure from watching others. In the more expensive forms of equine entertainment, such as racing, polo and eventing, you can have the added thrill of paying someone to do it for you.

To the British, the horse is not considered a sport but a religion.

## BADMINTON

'I am not fond of horses,' wrote the late Lord Ballantrae. 'My regard for them has slightly increased (I enjoy saying this) ever since I ate my charger in 1943, when I was hungry.' He enjoyed saying it, of course, because he knew that it would irritate almost everyone who read his book; in the national consciousness, the horse looms large.

'A thruster, a hard man to hounds, a good judge of horse-flesh,' are not quotations from a Regency romance but modern terms of approval. Even if you are not one of these, you will still be expected to show some knowledge of, and interest in, the Horse. One particularly important equine venue, the Mecca of British horse lovers (and one presumes their horses), the glory of the British Horse Society, is the Horse Trial in April at Badminton, the home of the Duke of Beaufort. Founded in 1949 by the 10th Duke to train and select riders for the European and Olympic championships, it was the first British horse trial, and in spite of over one hundred successors on other ducal land or in the parks of mere Irish non-voting peers, it remains the premier event today. Every chubby child at Pony Club dreams of competing here on the rolling, by Royal Gloucestershire standards, turf, through the shaded woods, in front of the great house. If they do not compete, they and their parents certainly spectate, queueing for hours in Volvo Estates, filled with 2.4 children and 1.4 black labradors, on the roads behind the horse-boxes, filling every house, inn and hotel for miles around.

Eventful hostelries:

a. Badminton House – home of 11th Duke of Beaufort (David), by tradition a royal house party that has been headed by the Queen and the Queen Mother;

b. Gatcombe Park – home of HRH The Princess Anne, Mrs Mark Phillips and Captain Mark Phillips. Your fellow guests will all be competitors, so unless you too compete you are in for a dull time;

c. Highgrove – home of Miss Barbara Barnes and her charges, and their parents, the Prince and Princess of Wales – comfortable but not noted for its horse conversation;

d. Someone else's horse-box, if you have left it too late to book into an hotel (several years in advance) or a good house party (by the end of the previous Badminton).

Any three day event, but especially Badminton, is a severe test of horse, rider and spectator, all of whom have been preparing for at least nine months. For the spectator, it is a severe social test, the first hurdle being dress. Correct tenue is country tweeds, box-calf brogues and bowler hat. The trouble is that, dressed like this, you will be mistaken for a dressage judge or the course vet and expected to do things in an officer-like manner. Far better to wear almost anything under a green Husky or Barbour and Hunter wellingtons; expensive scarf or flat cap are optional extras for women. You will then be indistinguishable from thousands of competitors, grooms (trying to look like competitors) and spectators (succeeding in looking like grooms) and be able to appear knowledgeable without embarrassment or responsibility.

Until the despairing cries of the head gardener (alias the Dowager Duchess of Beaufort) were heeded in 1959, the dressage on the first day was held on the lawn in front of the house. Now it has been moved and surrounded by tents, where host, royalty and judges sit enthroned like colonial governors. Nod to the Duke on the wagon (physical, not metaphorical). There are two opinions about dressage – the modern and the old-fashioned. The first holds that dressage is a proper test of a supple, obedient and well-trained animal; the second that it is a damn'd unEnglish way to ride a horse. Either way, enjoy the precise flow of the swallow-tailed, top-hatted riders executing the nineteen movements with the appropriate aids (this does not stand for 'acquired immune deficiency syndrome'). Since the marking system is a mystery to everyone with the possible exception of the judges, you can greet each score with well-bred scorn or sage approval, until it is time to walk the course.

The competitors must walk the cross-country course, probably several times, to discover:

a. where they are going;
b. by which of several unattractive routes they will approach each formidable jump.

You will walk the course:

a. because everyone does – avoid sitting on jumps as more often than not they have just received a fresh coat of creosote;
b. to have something to talk about at dinner – sprinkle your conversation with 'quite straightforward', or describe any jump that is considered difficult as 'a rider problem';
c. to discover which jump is nearest the bar;
d. to meet people.

People to meet:

a. HRH the Princess Anne, Mrs Mark Phillips;
b. Captain Mark Phillips;
c. Master Peter Phillips;
d. Miss Zara Phillips;
e. their grandmothers (both sides);
f. Mrs Green – Lucinda Prior-Palmer for it is she;
g. Richard Meade – looking preoccupied;
h. Lt-Colonel Frank Weldon – who will also be looking preoccupied since he designed the course;
i. Alison Oliver – who will also be looking preoccupied since she trained many of the competitors;
j. Minto Wilson – who will criticize the design arrangements and facilities and take you off to have a drink.

Before you go, you should choose your vantage point for the second day's events. Either keep on the move to meet your friends or take the less energetic option and stand by an interesting jump, perhaps the Ski Jump, Horsens Bridge or the Lamb Creep. Best of all, choose one with a jump judge you know to have a well-stocked Range Rover because, while the competitors will be careering past at ten-minute intervals, stop watches on wrist and a metronome ticking in their heads, you are going to have to sustain a day of horsey conversation.

Remarks you will overhear or, if brave enough, will make:

a. he/she is overriding the poor animal. English translation – The rider is inexperienced;
b. he/she is overfacing the poor animal. English translation – The rider's horse is inexperienced;
c. if he/she approaches the Pig Sty like that, he/she will run out/fall out. English translation – The rider is about to collect penalties, be disqualified or fall off.
d. bit of a bounce up hill over that one. English translation – The rider will certainly fall off.

Criticism should be directed at the competitors, the fences or their designer. If you must criticize a horse, describe it as 'nappy', an affectionate term for what anyone else would call bad-tempered, ill-mannered and thoroughly disobedient.

Conversation subjects to avoid:

a. 1966 – Badminton was rained off;
b. 1951 – the Swiss won.

Behaviour to avoid:

a. ignoring the warning whistle;
b. shouting encouragement/advice at HRH or indeed any competitor you happen to know;
c. letting your dog off the lead (especially if related to HRH Princess Anne, Mrs Mark Phillip's lurcher, Lulu);
d. chatting up the girl grooms – they won't speak to you if you are not on a horse anyway;
e. chatting up the male grooms – they may well speak to you if you are not on a horse.

Being a knowledgeable spectator is almost as exhausting as competing.

If the second day is the most physically testing for the horse and rider, and the most popular with the crowds at the water-jump, all waiting for Princess Anne to fall in (whether she is competing or not), the start of the third day finds the surviving competitors at their most nervous. Two days' marks are up; the leaders, often closely bunched together, are known; there is only the show-jumping left, where a tenth of a second or a nudged rail can collapse years of effort and hope. Be prepared to commiserate with failure, congratulate success and watch the jump-off. And then? The cups, the speeches and the glory; the chaos in the car park, the endless post-mortems on the course ('The Bull Pens were a sod, almost pre-Olympic') and your quiet angling for invitations to Wyley and Burghley, for even if you secretly agree with Lord Ballantrae you have discovered one thing: joining the event world is a far better introduction to society than the London Season.

## THE CHELTENHAM NATIONAL HUNT FESTIVAL

'Horses for courses, but keep your best horses for Cheltenham,' say the jumping trainers about that three-day National Hunt

Festival meeting held each March. National Hunt racing is a truly British sport now copied elsewhere, as in the New England states and New Zealand, and can be distinguished from the smarter flat racing by that pungent whiff of amateurism so beloved of the British of all classes. Whether it evolved from midnight chases across country or as an extension of hunting is immaterial to the gentleman jockeys and the professionals who risk life and limb every season, to the trainers who could make five times the amount on the flat, or to the average owner who stands an 11 to 1 chance of covering his costs.

The Cheltenham Festival is a blend of superlatives. There you will find:

a. the best racing in the National Hunt calendar, with the best horses brought to their peak to race for the richest prize-money – particularly the Irish challengers who own and train their horses with *only* Cheltenham in mind;

b. a combination of good horses and rich pickings attracting the most serious punters;

c. the greatest crowd of dedicated followers of National Hunt racing from both sides of the Irish Sea, hence

d. the worst traffic – it can take anything up to two hours to get on to the course – time spent in the reconnaissance of the back roads is never wasted. Alternatively, you can come by helicopter (like Captain Fred Barker MFH or Douglas Bunn of Hickstead fame) or sometimes a small aeroplane. Some come by train (the kippers and Buck's Fizz brigade), even by the Orient Express, but there you can never guarantee your fellow passengers unless you take a whole carriage;

e. the dirtiest weather, although no one seems deterred by Arctic conditions. Undeniably the best jump meeting, Cheltenham is not sartorially smart and you will find sheepskin coats, fur coats and hats, covert coats (the 't' is silent as in Harlow), brown felt hats and anything else that is warm. The fashionable suffer for their elegance although the new stands are a comfort to them.

Once you have made it on to the course, you should repair to the Turf Club tent for lunch. Although it is a fairly recent innovation, it has already become an integral part of the Meeting and the Mecca of the racing elite, mercifully including women. You can, of course, be invited to the Jockey Club Box, or the Stewards' Box where you will have a standard lunch and a great view of the racing, but it is more fun with the Turf crowd. Like the price of champagne, around £35 a bottle, the size of the tent is increasing annually.

The moving forces behind the Turf tent are Lord Vestey and Lord Hartington. The running of the tent is left to the Club's barman, Jimmy, who repels name-dropping intruders with a respectful gusto that comes from years of club service. Lunch is a feast, particularly if you like fish. Barry Cope, who does the catering, produces lobsters, crab and prawns fit for Neptune.

You can stay all day in the tent (judging by the number of champagne bottles on the tables, more than a few do), watch the racing on the four televisions and lay your bets with the resident bookmaker. You will meet many of the trainers and jockeys, particularly the gent' jockeys, and a good number of the owners. You may even have the chance to ask Sheikh Ali Abu Khamsin, who uncharacteristically prefers National Hunt Racing to the sleeker thrills of the flat, if he intends to build a stand at Chelten-ham like the one he has on the Devon and Exeter course – if so, latch on. You will meet a few of the flat race trainers and jockeys who, because of the superlative racing, deign to brave the cold and the crowds during their off season. You may also recognize Bryan Ferry or Charlie Watts of the Rolling Stones – as someone else's guest.

But whatever the delights of the Turf tent, it is not the true Cheltenham. To flavour the spirit of the meeting, you should venture to the paddock and the stands, and the bars after the race. There you will find the county set mingling happily with a huge Irish contingent, determined to disprove the saying that, 'three days is a long time to be riotous or drunk or both' as they wedel between the bar and a Guinness and the Irish Linen Bank to change some more punts if the Irish horses are doing badly. You will also rub shoulders with more Irish priests than if you had joined a seminary.

As you clutch your hat, your timeform and *The Sporting Life* against the blinding hail on your way to the paddock, you may well stumble across:

a. the Queen Mother – all pastel shades, galoshes and knowledge with her trainer, Fulke Walwyn;
b. the Prince and Princess of Wales – he passionately keen on race-riding, she patently less so;
c. The women trainers – Mrs Monica Dickinson, Mrs Jenny Pitman and Mrs Mercy Rimell – all hoping to out-distance their male rivels;
d. Nicky Henderson, looking for another good Cheltenham;
e. Charlie Benson, alias the Scout in the *Daily Express*, looking cheerful and confident because, after an extremely good lunch, he still believes that his nap selection will win;
f. Steve Smith-Eccles looking to repeat his 1985 form – the Ritz Trophy for the top jockey, not his shining black eye;
g. Dick Francis, looking for the plot of his next best seller;
h. Jim Wilson, the gifted amateur, with a long face despite the fact that he usually does well on his home course;
i. 'J P' McManus about to lay a massive wager;
j. any of the Irish priests as they laugh their way to the grandstand having placed their Easter offering on a hot tip on the 3.35 and none of them can lose, can they now?

As you watch the racing from high up in the grandstand, it is not difficult to see why Cheltenham is rated so highly. It is a beautiful course set in a bowl at the foot of Cleeve Hill. It is also a testing course for horse and rider, with stiff fences and a steep uphill climb from the last fence to the finishing post – many a horse has led over the last and not been placed on the run-in. Because of the importance of the meeting, the stewards will only abandon racing under the most extreme conditions and it is not uncommon to see the horses splashing through water far out 'in the country'.

If you are feeling strong enough, you can go to one of the many bars and fight for a drink. While being jostled and elbowed, you will hear a new language:

a. he gave him a lot to do – Anglo-Irish. Translation: the jockey left it too late to make a challenge;
b. he made too much use of the horse – Anglo-Irish. Translation: the jockey came too early to sustain his lead;

c. he came on a ton – Anglo-Irish. Translation: the horse was 'cheating' all season and won at Cheltenham, heavily backed at a good price.

Win or lose, you can not fail to have been infected with the magic of The Cheltenham National Hunt Festival. There is an adage that we are all equal above and below the turf; that was, however, before the advent of the Turf Club tent.

## ROYAL ASCOT

It is not for nothing that it is called Royal Ascot and is dubbed the most senior of all race meetings. For close on three hundred years, the Meeting has been patronized by the Royal Family – Queen Anne started it – and they (including its non-racing members) still attend in droves. Although the racing is the best of the flat season with the richest prize money, the quality of those in the Royal Enclosure has sadly declined. To the chagrin of the serious racing fraternity, the Royal Meeting has sunk to the level of a fashion parade. However, there is an inner sanctum within that Royal Enclosure, the Royal Box, which is a haven from the overcrowded lawns outside. You can attend that select gathering if you are a member of any of the Royal Family's Household, a perquisite of the job, or as a guest of Her Majesty the Queen. The Queen's house parties at Windsor Castle at Easter and for Ascot Week are the nearest that the Queen comes to 'holding Court' in the proper sense of the word, and this invitation is the most prestigious of any, at any time, in any year.

Your invitation, written on the heaviest of crested paper in a stampless envelope (franked E II R) that could not fail to impress the postman, will arrive some time in February. Once you receive and accept that letter from the Queen's Deputy Master of the Household, Lieutenant-Colonel Blair Stewart-Wilson, you are locked into the system. Later, he will solicit the names of your valet and/or ladies maid (both if there are two of you) and, if you have not grown up or stayed in a Royal house before, your pedal measurements as well (hopefully you will not need to borrow Royal wellies in the middle of June).

You will be advised to arrive at around six o'clock on the

Monday evening – the Royal Ascot meeting starts on Tuesday. The George IV Gate will be closed (that week, the Castle is out of court to paying visitors) but a policeman, armed with the number of your car, will breathe the right Sesame for the gates to open. Follow the line of cars with the coats of arms on the door and the race-horse mascots on the bonnet (the *cognoscenti* can place the occupants behind smoked glass from the cyphers or the racing colours) up to the Sovereign's Entrance (the size of a modest house) and proceed inside, where a liveried footman will take charge of you – the Queen does not meet her guests at the door, whoever they are, so do not be put out. Most likely you are in for a long walk to your room, as are your valet and ladies maid, who have to remember not only their own layout but yours as well. During the lengthy hike down chill corridors, draughty even in June, pause to think what it is like behind those thirteen-foot walls in winter. Your rooms may prove to be a disappointment, as at Windsor some of the guests' bedrooms, although comfortable, are far from grand. However, they will be 'personalized'. Well before your arrival, a bevvy of pretty girls in the Royal library will have researched your more proper interests and your background, and furnished your room with appropriate pictures and *objets d'art* from the Royal collection. The Queen will have inspected it herself to make sure all is well.

With luck, your valet and/or ladies maid will have found your room and brought your clothes, (black tie) suitably pressed (note for servants: take an adaptor for the iron, the plugs are all the old-fashioned round-pin variety). Before half past seven, you will be called by your own friendly footman, who knows his way about the place, and escorted to the Green Drawing Room to meet the Queen, Prince Philip and the other members of the Royal Family who are staying, which will be most of them. You will also meet the other guests, anything up to forty, although the majority will not actually be staying in the Castle. There are masses of relations, who happen to be friends, members of the various Royal Households, who also happen to be friends, and friends, who happen to share their interests, like humour and racing and racing and racing. Time spent with *Burkes* on the pages marked 'Royal Household' and with *The Sporting Life* will not be wasted.

Other likely guests:

a. a pride of Bowes Lyon,
b. a neiveful of Neville,
c. a knitch of Knatchbull,
d. a hurtle of Herbert,
e. a flurry of Fane,
f. an ogle of Ogilvy,
g. an accretion of Anson,
h. a haras of Halifax,
i. any number of *von und zu's* and the token foreign dignitaries.

When meeting the Queen, women cannot curtsey too low (practise first, for if you fall over it will upset you more than it amuses them). Leave the bow from the waist to the head waiter, those who know drop the head forward sharply like a cleanly shot pheasant (known as a Coburg bow). The Queen, as other members of the Royal Family, will take your hand somewhere by your thumb. Experience from many Royal filleted digits dexter has taught them to strike first (like the corgis). It is easier if you like champagne but do not try to guess the vintage.

Although the evening is informal, dinner is nonetheless a grand affair. You will be told where you are sitting, your chair will be drawn back by the footman and you are ready to embark on the first of many Royal dinners. At home, the Duke of Edinburgh exercises his paternal rights as head of the family and engages his end of the table in high sounding talk – a working knowledge of his book, *Men, Machines and Sacred Cows* will be useful.

Food: little, rich and often. Do not be surprised that the Queen may have different food from the rest of the dinner party, she sometimes finds the food too rich and refuses to suffer for your pleasure. Being served first, she will most likely have finished before you start.
Drink: Ibid.
Conversation:

a. on the Queen's side:
   i. very serious racing
   ii. the progeny of Aureole
   iii. homeopathy of Aureole
   iv. homeopathy

    v. the progeny of Highclere (little, rich and often).
  b. on the Duke of Edinburgh's side:
    i. all horses save race horses
    ii. breeding of endangered animals
    iii. suppression of breeding among endangered humans
    iv. breeding – save race horses.

After dinner you will meet up again for further entertainment. The Royal Family are very much a family and their brand of entertainment and their wit is 'in Castle'. They are all accomplished mimics and have been acting since the nursery. In-castle entertainment is of a high standard:

  a. the game – have stock of subjects ready, not the Queen's favourites, *Forever Amber*, *les liaisons dangereuses*, Aureole;
  b. tour of the private apartments, guide: HM The Queen;
  c. jigsaws – best left to the Queen, never do a Queen Mary, forcing the pieces unless they fit.

Do not sneak off to bed before any of the Royal Family, unless specifically invited to do so.

  For those unused to Castle life, *pace* Nancy Mitford, your day will not hang heavy and, like your five changes of clothes, will be laid out for you with almost military precision.

0730 hrs  Awoken by Queen's pipe major – far more effective than Wogan
0830 hrs  breakfast in the Oak Breakfast Room – *sans* major Royals but still leave the last devilled kidney just in case
0915 hrs  change into riding clothes
0930 hrs  traditional ride round the course – hopefully your mount has retired from active racing for quite some time. Note: do not remark on the early start to the Queen who has already done her boxes (even during Ascot week). Do not ask what is in them, she won't tell
1030 hrs  free time
1031 hrs  change and play tennis. Standard high, particularly Princess Anne and Prince Andrew. Alternatively, escape to antique shop in Windsor

| 1200 hrs | Change for the races – if morning coat too small say had it since school – presupposes still elegant old Etonian |
| 1229 hrs | Take sea-sick pills (the R F swears by Kwells) as carriages sway horribly |
| 1230 hrs | Light lunch |
| 1330 hrs | Enter Ascot Landaus (pronounced landor) |

With luck you will be in one of the five carriages – not the first as that is reserved for the Queen, Prince Philip and the Master of the Horse, the Earl of Westmorland. Do not be tempted to wave, it is a Royal prerogative and they have had so much more practice. Ignore, or try to ignore, equine flatulence. A discreet nod to one of your friends is permissible. Those not in carriages go up the course by car which, while not nearly so exciting or socially exposed, does make the Kwells redundant.

Once in the Royal Stand, you will be surrounded by many of those at dinner the night before and their pretty daughters/sons. Identification is mercifully easier as by now they are all wearing their distinctive Royal Household Badges with their names (except the Royal Family and if you can not recognize them by now, go straight to the White's tent and do not come back). Make sure that you have yours. Even the Princess of Wales, as Lady Diana Spencer, without her badge and detached from the Royal Party, was hard pressed to return to the Royal Box – the yeoman pricker (sic for it is he) was deaf to her entreaties until rescued by her fiancé.

The Royal Stand is furnished like a university's London club, with no more than passable pictures, chairs and sofas, but it is perfectly adequate for all that and, if you glance at the 'privileged' crowds outside, a haven for a week's racing.

Courtier points:

a. cheering in a Royal winner – it lifts the party no end;
b. escorting the Queen down the funnel to the paddock, but not too often;
c. congratulating Lester Piggot on yet another win (little, rich and often);
d. decorously discussing your schooldays with Robert Fellowes – do not refer to him by his old nick-name 'Bertie', rather too close to home in Royal Circles;

e. decorously discussing your schooldays with the Princess of Wales;
f. being decorous.

*Lèse majesté:*

a. entering the Royal ante-room reserved for the Royal Family;
b. cheering anything but a Royal winner – dangerous as many of the Household, and most of the guests will own, or train, many of the horses running and although they will not say they mind, they will;
c. offering to lay the Queen a good price on the next race;
d. switching channels of television to Play School, even if implored by the Princess of Wales;
e. smoking.

Lesser sin: joining the Prince of Wales as he sneaks off to play polo.

When time to go, you may be lucky enough to be asked back to Royal Lodge for tea – taken with Queen Elizabeth it will probably be 70 degrees proof (little, rich and often). Conversation will revolve round people rather more than horses – while the Queen is an expert on flat racing, Queen Elizabeth prefers National Hunt. Solicit a walk round the gardens, which are magnificent at that time of year. Come armed with the latin names of a few rare species of rhododendrons to weave into your conversation. All too quickly, it will be time to return to the Castle, across the Great Park. As you enter, it will be 1830 hrs, and, in the refrain of the song that you may well sing after dinner, 'It's Starting All Over Again'.

## POLO

High up in the foothills of the Himalayas, close to one of the earliest polo grounds, an early groupie has carved on a now weather-beaten board:

'Let other men do other things
The King of Sports is the Sport of Kings'

Several centuries later and more down to earth, the equine

correspondents of their day, Sellars and Yeatman, described polo as 'a lofty species of horse-croquet invented by the Lofty Maharajahs of India, or possibly the Shifty Shaherezadjahs of Perzhia, or possibly by the Chinese during the p'ing p'ong dynasty – we don't know – but the point is, polo has always been the only exclusively aristocratic pastime, limited to the best people (*chukkah-sahibs* and all those) and played most exclusively at the other end of the ground so that the Common People shall never comprehend it.' It all depends on your vantage point, high up in the stands, or looking over, under or away from your pony, as to which view you take of the game. Few sports can rival top class polo – known by the boards (that surround the ground) as high-goal polo – played on a sunny, warm day in an exquisite park, for excitement and beauty. No sport in the world can rival bad polo, played on a wet, cold afternoon for utter misery. Not surprisingly, the spectators think so too.

You can watch good high-goal polo at three grounds – all different in style, players and spectators. In Royal Gloucestershire there is Cirencester where Capability Brown had the foresight to allow for two beautiful, manicured grounds surrounded by tall beeches and chestnut when he laid out the park. There the players are rich and the spectators blend well with the surroundings. At Windsor Great Park, the Guards' Polo Club grounds are more regal than beautiful, the players mixed, and the spectators have been described as 'piss elegant with wrought iron voices'. After the early tournaments in June at Windsor and Cirencester, the high goal teams centre on Cowdray, near Midhurst, in the near-side of Sussex, for the rest of the season. Cowdray is indeed blessed with everything – beautiful grounds complete with Eliza-bethan ruin; Lord Cowdray, a rich and enthusiastic patron of the game; and a hard core of loyal spectators. If you are not sitting with Lord Cowdray in his fenced-off enclosure, you will be high up in the stands (which also affords a grander view).

Your fellow spectators will include:

a. former polo players too old or too poor to play;
b. young hopefuls anxious to be noticed by a patron;
c. their sisters also hoping to be noticed;
d. attentive polo wives (in the minority);
e. inattentive polo wives, children and obligatory assortment of black labradors and Jack Russell terriers.

Unlike most traditionally English equestrian sports, you can dress exactly as you like and still not be out of place. However, most spectators will be dressed identically, regardless of age, with the men in battered straw hats with a Brigade of Guards or Eton hat band, tie with obligatory tie pin, frayed shirt, flannel trousers and heavy brown brogues or chukka boots (for treading in). Their wives/girl-friends/sisters all dress like the Princess of Wales, who has made a study of sitting at the side of a polo ground – 'summer frock', pearls, regimental brooch and sensible flat shoes (also for treading in). You can then settle down to watch the polo. You do not have to have any special skills to do so, although the fact that the players change ends after each goal can be confusing.

The better the polo, the less the shouting and swearing, although more than the odd mild rebuke does slip out from time to time. At half time, after two chukkas (three in high goal), it is time for the ritualistic treading in – the reason for the brogues, chukka boots and sensible flat shoes – when spectators from both sides of the ground mingle in a classless sea of stamping feet over divots and hoof prints. (Even the Queen goes treading in, which swells the sea of classless spectators.)

After the final chukka comes the presentation of the cup and the obligatory magnum of champagne. Fortunately, polo is not like the end of a motor racing grand prix where the crowd is sprayed with champagne, so there is always plenty to drink. After this ceremony, talk to the winning captain, who will doubtless try to convert you into becoming a polo player.

To those who play, the game is undeniably 'the king of sports', although the 'sport of kings' is a little wide of the mark in Britain, save of course for the Heir Apparent and the Malay royal family. You are more likely to meet barons, meat barons, manufacturers (paint and biscuits) and dealers (pictures, bronzes and arms) than even a deposed king from a minor European Court.

High goal polo is very, very expensive unless you happen to be a top class player, when it is very, very lucrative, which is part of the reason why top class polo is very, very expensive. If you are a reasonable player, you may be asked to play for one of the high goal teams. You will soon realize that your presence in the team is due to your indigenous status rather than any special skill (only two out of the four players can be foreigners). You will be shouted at continually by:

a. the sponsor;
b. the professionals;
c. the grooms;

unless you also happen to be the Heir Apparent when you are still shouted at but the outburst is mildly tempered by 'Sir'.
If you:

a. do not like being shouted at;
b. like shouting at others;
c. like playing your own ponies;
d. do not mind sharing your best ponies and/or wife with your professionals;

you are probably better off (not financially) running your own team. For this you will need:

a. money and plenty of it, say £75,000 for the year's expenses;
b. a high enough handicap, at least two – in polo, handicaps are rated from minus two to ten (unlike golf, ten is the best). For high goal polo, the combined team handicaps must be over sixteen so the lower your handicap, the more you will have to pay for hirelings to play with you (their fees are commensurate with their handicaps);
c. an endless string of polo ponies – not really ponies at all, but thoroughbred, super-fast horses that would be equally at home on the racecourse, sometimes crossed with hot, nippy Argentine blood so they turn quicker. As you will be mounting your team, allow for twenty ponies and a great deal of money – say an average of £5000 a pony;
d. an establishment that can accommodate these twenty ponies and the grooms and the horseboxes and the team and their cars (provided by you) and the interminable barbecues that go with polo;
e. a polo wife who is beautiful enough to keep the hired as-sassins happy (however, since the Falklands and the absence of the Argentinians (Argis) from the polo scene, this is of less importance. The Argentinians have now largely been replaced by New Zealand, Peruvian, Chilean and Brazilian players who are, so far, less demanding. Polo wives come expensive;

f. time – to reach the required standard to play in high goal matches means that you have to devote your life to polo (at least in the early stages). This in turn means going abroad to play in the winter as well as in Europe all summer for years and years, which means of course, spending a great deal of money.

It will be useful to have a polo manager to do the endless chores connected with running a high goal polo team. He could well come from that breed of impecunious ex-cavalry officers, retired for unspecified reasons before their time, who will take on the job (or that of one of the smaller polo club managers) in return for a few crumbs from your table, such as the odd chukka, a meagre salary or a damp cottage. Thus set up with your team in a rented house and stables near Midhurst, you can indulge yourself in an orgy of high goal polo all summer, a season of tournaments and matches that culminates in The British Open Polo Championship which includes the Gold Cup.

Popular Polo Patrons' teams:

a. Lord Cowdray's Cowdray Park – still somewhat of a family team including his son, the Hon. Charles Pearson (a promising player currently in the amusement business);
b. Guy Wildenstein's *Les Diables Bleus* – a very senior team with the Prince of Wales, the Brazilian Carlos Gracida, and his groom, Jesus;
c. Galen Weston's Maple Leafs – Canadian buiscuit and supermarket money fund a team that includes one of the top English players, Julian Hipwood;
d. The Davids Jamieson and Yoeman's Southfields – strong favourites to win everything with a team that includes the hirsute Alan Kent;
e. Nicky Hahn's *Ingwenya* – the Zulu crocodile team with Howard Hipwood, the other top English player, easily recognized from the pages of the glossy magazines as *the* polo-playing male model;

High goal polo is a game to be played with hot blood and a cool head. Once your match begins, all your effort, practice and cash is put to the test. It is forty-five minutes (six chukkas with a breather between each) of flashing sticks, galloping ponies, curses, bumps and consummate skill. It is a mixture of riding expertise and tactics where luck plays a very small part. At the end of the game, you shake hands with the opposition, pat your pony and kiss the wife of the sponsor of the tournament.

If you win an important race with an expensive race horse, you at least have some return in prize money and breeding potential. With polo, at the end of the successful day, all you end up with is a bottle of champagne, an engraved glass or a jar of tea. At the end of the season, probably all you have to show for your considerable outlay is an ashtray engraved with a polo scene, too small to be of any use.

## HUNTING

'Adultery hung heavy over Melton Mowbray.' This is hardly the opening line of a Foxford hunting report in *Horse and Hound* but describes the extra- and intra-mural activities of a high proportion of fox-hunting folk during their season, around that meta-centre of their world in the heart of England. This world is the Quorn, Cottesmore and Belvoir Hunts and the rolling countryside of High Leicestershire, the same that has provided sport for generations of 'jolly gentlemen in coats of red' and their ladies since Stuart times. Each generation since has much in common, in that it complains that the country is not what it used to be before:

a. the Civil War;
b. the early Hanoverians (although George III was a passionate hunting man);
c. the railways (let in the wrong sort of people from London);
d. the Great War (ploughing up that rolling grassland);
e. the Hitler War (more ploughing up that rolling grassland);
f. helicopters (for the same reasons as c.).

Despite the said interruptions and degeneracy, packs of hounds in England, especially the Melton Packs, have not only thrived but have a waiting list of subscribers. Hunting is still an essential part of English life (unless you happen to be a fox when it can be decidedly unhealthy) because:

a. it separates
  i. the bold from the timid
  ii. the Shire thrusters (they are also called 'Melton Blades')
     from the lavender cowboys
b. it unites
  i. men/women with nature
  ii. men/women with their horses
  iii. men/women with each other
c. it is an opportunity
  i. to dress up
  ii. to show off
  iii. to participate in one of the fastest and most thrillin' of all
      field sports

Before you can begin to 'cut a dash' sartorially, it helps if you can ride well (most of the county who hunt have ridden since the day of conception, but more on that later). Hunting clothes could have been designed with only the vain in mind, so it is essential not to let them, or your horse, down.

Once you are a subscriber you will be allowed to wear a 'red' coat (the *cognoscenti* call them scarlet, the uninitiated call them red, while the pedantic stick to pink after the nineteenth century hunting tailor). In the tradition of nature, it is only the cock-bird that is allowed the bright plumage – unless the female of the species is counted as an honorary male when she is given a courtesy title as Master of Foxhounds and although she can not wear the red, she is allowed the doubtful privilege of adding brass buttons to her blue coat. A greater honour than wearing red is to be awarded your hunt button. This is at the discretion of the Master for service in the field and comes after years of fawning on him, making large contributions to the hunt fund, opening gates, walking hound puppies or owning vast tracts of grassland in 'the country'. If you are not a subscriber, it is best to go for a black swallow-tail coat and breeches from:

a. Frank Hall of Market Harborough (known as F 'all), breeches
   a speciality – if you are very rich;
b. Savile Row – Huntsman is, and sounds, about right if you
   are very, very rich;

c. Mr Frazer at Hospital in Tipperary where you will not only
have your clothes made cheaper and better but will also have
a complete run-down of his clients that reads like a cross
between *Bailey's Hunting Directory* and *Burke's Peerage*;
d. Mr Bird from Leicester or Mr Gorringe from Walsall. Amazingly, there are more saddlers in Walsall than pubs in Melton.

To complete your hunting kit, have a pair of boots made at
Maxwell's (£860 and £164 for trees – allow eighteen weeks for
delivery) and a hard top hat or cap from Locks or Herbert Johnstone (Mr Patey from the Elephant and Castle is cheaper and
provides the same item). Since the top hat is solely for show and
no earthly use in a fall (an expensive concertina), you are now
allowed to wear a grey hunting cap with your scarlet coat – some
have been wearing them for years but then they are grey with age
rather than the 'new fad'. It may not be many years before the
top hat is a memory in the hunting field like the old-fashioned
stove-pipe hat. A useful tip to your valet is that, as you can no
longer buy a silk top hat, he can make your felt one look like silk
by the judicious use of Guinness applied with a sponge.

There are still a few other essential items of dress required
before you are ready to move off:

a. tights – for men and women, very warm and help to slip
your boots on and off – can be awkward for men to buy/try
on and even more difficult to explain if taken to hospital
unconscious after a bad fall;
b. Smedley (even Damart) underwear – men and women, helps
to combat the inevitable cold;
c. false buns – women only;
d. gold stock-pin, straight bar only;
e. gold safety pins (curved) for stock, breeches etc;
f. handkerchief – saves the back of your glove.

Looking every inch the son/daughter of Surtees, you need a
horse to match. To keep up with the Quorn you must have
something pretty classy and you can count yourself fortunate if
you can persuade either of those legendary horse-copers, George
Coombe or Dr Tom Connors, to find you a mount. When asked
about your horse, whatever the make, reply, 'It's Irish three-

quarter bred by a well known stallion out of a useful mare', and heads will nod with approval.

Other horses will include:

a. solid pure-bred Irish heavyweight hunters ridden by solid less pure-bred heavyweight hunters;
b. light thoroughbreds ridden by light thoroughbred gels;
c. light draught horses from the King's Troop, Royal Horse Artillery, ridden by light-weight officers;
d. heavy army horses from the Household Cavalry. As with c., both lots of horses are supposedly recovering from the London season (like their riders) at the Remount Depot, Melton Mowbray;
d. farmers' cobs;
e. Pony Club 'Thelwell' ponies.

In hunting parlance, you do not live in a village or near one, but in a specific country – 'Quorn Monday', 'Quorn Friday' or 'Cottesmore Tuesday' – there is even a large part of Oxfordshire, known as 'Bicestershire' that corresponds with the Bicester and Warden Hill's hunting country. Your hunting interlocutor will know where you live far more accurately than if you say 'off the B1709 by the Shell service station'. These country references are venues for 'the meet', Quorn Mondays and Fridays are the smartest with anything up to five hundred mounted followers and the bitch pack. Some consider Quorn Tuesdays and Saturdays with the dog pack are more enjoyable, with the genuine hunting folk and fewer scarlet coats. Meets are sometimes on the village green, or at some grand house when it is called a 'lawn meet'. The name is misleading. If you put so much as a hoof on the aforesaid lawn, you are liable to be sent home before you start. Village greens, however, are fair game. That said, you mostly meet in a draughty field where you mill round as at the start of the Grand National. There you meet the rest of the field (another misleading term as it refers to the mounted followers rather than anything agricultural). Quorn huntin' folk to be recognized by:

a. the Joint Masters, Joss Hanbury, Jim Bealby and Barry Hancock;
b. the hunt servants – Michael Farrin, huntsman, and the whippers-in Charlie Watts and Michael Scott;

c. your wife's lover;
d. any of the grand old huntin' folk such as Lady Margaret Fortescue, Lord Manton, the Hon. Ursula (Urkie) Newton, the Hon. Migs Greenhall, 'The Chairman' Lord King BA, Colonel Carplease-Martin L.L., and not least
f. The Prince of Wales (he is not in fancy dress, his blue coat with red facings is the George III Windsor uniform).

People not to be recognized by:

a. your husband's mistress;
b. the secretary, Major Charlie Humfrey, to cap you (expensive) £60 for the day – if you are a subscriber, your subscription of £750 will cover you for one day a week for the season;
c. anyone improperly dressed (except a farmer);
d. the hound puppy you walked (brought up) the year before.

Meety conversation:

a. the development of old affairs during the last week;
b. prospect of new affairs next week;
c. barley kids – the ones (like spring barley) that take four months to mature after marriage. Children ideally should be conceived during Smithfield Week, the first week of December, so as not to lose a day's hunting during this or next season (for polo-playing women, they should conceive during the week of the Royal Show [early June]);
d. the day, as in good/bad scenting day, a reference to the weather rather than the lavender cowboys' aftershave;
e. the 'FPT' (the forward pelvic thrust) of the saddle for women that is thought to be the cause of the high promiscuity rate in the horse world.
f. music, as in hound music to the ears;
g. performance of the bitch pack, not a pejorative term describing those on light thoroughbreds after those on Remount horses, but of hounds – bitches are faster than dog hounds anyway;
h. performance of the Prince of Wales;
i. performance of people everyday hunting folk dislike:
    i. hunt saboteurs and the League Against Cruel Sports – the antis

   ii. the Labour Party - more antis

  iii. Patrick Moore – maintains that hunting is as bad for the hunter as the hunted.

Conversations to avoid:

  a. none.

Some time around eleven, hounds move off, led by the huntsman, with the two whippers-in and the field master. From then on it is the survival of the pushiest on the best horses. While the huntsman is busy executing a number of exercises to find a fox to hunt, you will be kept in check by the field master so that you do not interfere with the huntsman, hunt servants or hounds (remember no definite article where hounds are concerned). If a fox is not forthcoming and there is too much trotting on the roads, then the huntsman will invent a fox (although he will never admit it) and lead the field for a 'lark' over the most interesting country – on a social day, the majority of the field will not realize and will care even less.

While the huntsman is drawing a covert, putting hounds through a wood to flush out a fox (who is no doubt wondering why the door to his earth has been filled in with earth by an earth-stopper the night before), it is time to keep quiet – only hounds are allowed to speak.

Once 'hounds have found' and are running, you are off. Unless right up at the front, you will see precious little because of:

  a. mud in your eyes;
  b. steam from everyone else's horses when you check;
  c. everybody else's elbows;
  d. stopping to catch the Prince of Wales's loose horse.

If you do make it to the front, like most other thrusters who have cut into the side of fences in front of a queue waiting to jump and sent women and children (worse, their horses too) into raging torrents off bridges, there is an even more important code to follow. Failure to avoid certain excesses will have you sent home:

  a. riding over a hound, even if it is the one you walked and you want revenge for the ravages to your chickens and your life;

b. jumping fences for fun when hounds are not running, particularly into seed fields – this tends to incur the displeasure of the farmer over whose land you are hunting;

c. passing the field master, huntsman or other hunt servants or hounds, particularly if they are about to draw a new covert or hounds have checked – the fox will be pleased, but no one else.

It is not too long, however, before the field thins out and the townies and antis have had enough and gone home. The real hunting then starts and with luck you will be in need of your second horse, which your groom/livery stable, being psychically aware of the fox's movements, will have waiting for you. As you change over horses like a Pony Express rider, there may be time for a quick sandwich and a nip at your flask (the Belvoir stop for a drinks party for half an hour). Then you are off again until dusk, which you will recognize as the time when the Prince of Wales goes home.

Again, with luck, your groom has found you, so that you do not have the long, damp and chilly hack back to your box. But your day is still only half through. There follows the great hunting tea. The GHT is a combination of breakfast and tea, without the flakers but with the addition of whisky in your tea. It is very much of an institution. Even if you have not been able to keep up with hounds, you can at least keep up with the conversation, so that you can relate what it was like at the front over dinner – if you can face dinner after coddled eggs, boiled eggs, crumpets swimming in butter, brown bread and butter or toast, Gentleman's Relish, strawberry jam and cake: fruit, ginger or sponge and, best of all, chocolate.

When you return home or to where you are staying, you will sink into a hot, full bath, with whisky; then dinner with whisky afterwards. Watch out for the man who is not drinking whisky, he is probably after your wife.

# CHAPTER 5

# FOR THE LOVE OF THE GAME

To be good at games at school used to be the passport to popularity and the ticket to a good college at Oxbridge. Today sport is less pre-eminent, but it still counts. On leaving university, there are still many outlets (besides horsing around) for the gifted amateur sportsman to carry on being physical, such as cricket, tennis, sailing or the most sedentary of all pastimes, fishing. Most, however, find the time to combine their activities with spectating, the quiet approval of Lord's cricket, the bonk and swearing of Wimbledon tennis or even the soft propulsion of wood through water at Henley. Whether players or spectators, the British usually manage to turn their sport into a social occasion.

## CRICKET

Kipling wrote of cricketers as 'flanneled fools at the wicket'. There is no excuse for such an attitude (not even living in the Indian sub-continent for so long) for the world knows that cricket is the quintessence of England. It is sport in its purest form, the embodiment of all that painted the map of the world the colour of red on a fast bowler's flannels.

There is cricket, and there is cricket. On the one hand, there are the county sides which are made up of hired professionals. Their game bears the stigmata of sponsorship, advertising, bad manners and boardroom squabbles, even international incidents. On the other hand, there are tens of thousands of dedicated cricketers who every weekend make village greens throughout England resemble a James Pollard print of 'The Noble Game', and those people who are invited to play for one, or a combination, of the many private cricket clubs. Each club has its own particular bent: Jim Swanton's Arabs consider themselves a seriously good side; Lavinia, Duchess of Norfolk has a team of ex-county players in her name; David Nicholson picks his team from the racing world (they use the Queen Mother's racing colours); Richard Parsons runs a team from the wine trade; the Band of Brothers (originally made up of Leigh-Pembertons) come from Kent, while the Hampshire Hogs are more county than porcine. Army sides, like the Household Brigade in Burton Court, London, or the Green Jackets at Winchester, have their regimental bands playing during matches and the pleasures of the mess after. To the members of IZ, there is no greater honour than being invited to join, and play for, I Zingari.

Purists insist that it should be *Gli Zingari,* but then GZ does not have the same ring about it. I Zingari is the Italian for 'the gipsies' – an apt title for a cricket club which has never had a ground of its own and which wanders around playing clubs that have. Like many good British institutions (and people), it was conceived as the result of a good dinner. After a William Bolland had thrashed a side of Harrow schoolboys with his team in 1845, he invited three friends to dine at the Blenheim Hotel in New Bond Street, now the Tartan Shop. There, with the aid of much excellent claret and port, they decided to form a cricket club and formulated the rules – the vinous R. P. Long surfacing for just long enough to name the club. (The first minutes began, 'At a Meeting held – no matter when, and much less where – NOBODY, Chairman.) Some rules show spirit, such as Rule 6, 'That the Entrance be nothing, and the Annual Subscription do not exceed the Entrance, but the expenses of the match (i.e. of the Zingaric umpire, etc.) be defrayed by the Members engaged therein', or Rule 7, 'That all directions connected with the game *may* be conveyed in the French or Italian language.' With only minor changes, those rules apply today.

One rule, however, that has been changed is the third, by which prospective members were to be 'placed at the wicket, with or without a bat, as the officers [committee members] may decide and be bowled at by the AVP [Annual Vice President] or by any Member of IZ so deputed by the AVP. One straight ball to exclude . . .' Your invitation to join IZ is less of an ordeal; it will come in their discreetly embossed envelope and written on a good weight of paper with the IZ colours across the corner. The invitation comes because:

a. two of your closest chums have put your name forward to the committee for consideration (which two, you supposedly never know);
b. you already play for the Eton Ramblers, having captained the eleven while at that school, or similar – hence are a good cricketer;
c. you are a good chap – girls, of course are not tolerated as players (even if you are Rachel Heyhoe Flint or similar) – and so fit in with the camaraderie of your fellow subjects of King Willow.

On your grateful acceptance, you become a *sibene*, mercifully short for *Sibenesegesserint*. Before you can become a full playing member, you have to prove yourself on and off the field.

Sibene sins:

a. wearing the IZ colours, or indeed any Kerry Packer coloured shirt, jacket or trousers – *after* election it is frowned on if you wear another club's sweater when playing for IZ;
b. not keeping 'a promise to play';
c. using an aluminium bat or a cookabarro ball (Australian, with a single seam);
d. talking enthusiastically to Lady Becher, wife of IZ's secretary of long standing, Sir 'Billy' Becher;
e. not talking enthusiastically to Lady Becher;
f. proposing a toast to anybody.

Once Sir Billy has approved your performance, you are made a 'full-play member', the next category up is 'half-play member', then 'candidate for the asylum for the aged and decayed Zingari'. The only real difference you will find is that *sibenes* do not pay a match fee. IZ have a particularly garish set of colours: black, red and gold – 'out of darkness, through fire, into light' – always worn with the gold at the top unless you are in mourning for the Sovereign when black is worn uppermost. The legend goes that R. P. Long (remember him?) met a gipsy fortune teller in Spain who told him that he was going to found a famous cricket club and, so that he could tickle her palm with silver, she sold him her scarf with the racing colours of her particular tribe.

If you wish to look like a latter-day Jacob, Beale and Inman of New Bond Street will make you up a brand new blazer from the little cloth that they still hold. Alternatively, you may be given or inherit an IZ blazer, most likely aged, loved and spotted with port. Wear it with pride.

Women – wives, daughters and sisters of members – are also allowed to wear the club's colours, usually in expensive brooches. Perish the thought of them actually playing cricket but three women have been individually acknowledged. The Duchess of Kent is a Member and a Freeman of IZ, voted in as the daughter of Sir William Worsley (ex-Captain of Yorkshire) rather than for her Royal position; Lavinia, Duchess of Norfolk is also a Freeman through her late husband; while Mrs Robin Leigh-Pemberton is classed as an 'attachée'.

Suitably elected and attired, you are now open to offers from a team manager to play in his team. Team managers are chosen at the beginning of each season, allocated a match and asked to make up a side. All fixtures have their advantages, some greater than others. The South Wales Hunts give splendid house parties; Torry Hill, the home of the Band of Brothers and Robin Leigh-Pemberton, is an easy drive from London; Lavinia, Duchess of Norfolk's match is played at Arundel Castle and you get to see her legendary race horses and inside the Castle. Another cracking match is the one against Lord Porchester's eleven at his ground at Highclere, in Hampshire.

If you are playing against His Lordship's eleven, it is certain that you will not be staying with him for the weekend as he tends to put up his own team first. Gone are the days when most country houses had their own cricket pitches and teams made up of family, neighbours and staff, but Lord Porchester, a keen if not over-accomplished cricketer, has maintained both. It is a beautiful ground, with its thatched far pavilion, surrounded by tall beeches, rhododendrons, expensive cars and pretty girls. It has improved since Henry Herbert, Highclere's incumbent Hon.-in-waiting but one, formed his own team. The lunch is good too.

Lord Porchester's team will be made up of good cricketers, mostly members of IZ, such as Henry Wyndham and Simon Parker-Bowles, and the odd keen equine neighbour like Ian Balding, who sometimes captains the team when it is not run by Henry Herbert. The IZ team captain for the Highclere match is usually G. P. S. Delisle, a former Middlesex county player.

Senior players to choose from:

a. the Earl of Cottenham (Charlie) – demon fast bowler;
b. Stephen Willis – another ace bowler;
c. Sir Ian Collet – takes a good wicket;
d. Rupert Daniels – Eton and Oxford;
e. Charles Fry – Oxford and county player;
f. the Duke of Roxburgh – steady player;
g. Mike Griffiths – former captain of Sussex;
h. Sir 'Merve the Swerve' Dunnington Jefferson – despite his sobriquet, a steady spin bowler;
i. Mike Hooper – former Surrey player, useful bat;
j. David Baldry – a Hampshire county player;
k. Richard Hutton – Len's boy, played for Yorkshire;
l. Mark Faber – an old Sussex player.

Beneath that languid and gentlemanly air that surrounds every IZ cricket match, there is the deep-rooted will to win – the same can be said of the opposition, especially where Henry Herbert is concerned. Today, the standard of cricket is high, the off field spirits higher and the competition keener every year, something which the vinous R. P. Long would doubtless have approved. With IZ, *floruit, floret, florebit*.

LAST PLAYER

# CRICKET AT LORD'S

Where sport is concerned, foreigners are a jealous lot. The French believe that they invented real tennis and the Red Indians claim lacrosse, but nobody, absolutely nobody, can take the invention of cricket away from the English. Not only did the British invent cricket, they played it wherever they went (including Hollywood), and the game stuck, whether in Nigeria or on the ice of Iglodlick. As an inheritance of the Empire, the game is a bond between India and Pakistan, South Africa and the West Indies, Yorkshire County Cricket Club and whoever they may be currently quarrelling with. Although cricket can be savoured with pleasure throughout the former British Empire, nothing can compare with watching a match on its home ground at Lord's, the seat of the Marylebone Cricket Club in North London – as with foxhounds and Albany (one of the smartest addresses in London), there is no definite article before the initials 'MCC'.

It is not especially difficult to be elected a member of MCC – as with many such institutions, the need for money speaks louder than exclusivity. All you need is a proposer and seconder and it is not long before you are in. Armed with your snappy little red pass, you enter the hallowed grounds by the W. G. Grace Memorial Gate, give a 'footman's nod' to the gatekeeper, then make your way to the Pavilion. This is a splendid place for all lovers of cricket (as long as they are male). There you can wander round the passages and stairways, admiring walls set with pictures of every conceivable cricketer playing in every conceivable quarter of the world. The inner sanctum of Lord's is the Long Room which, as its name implies, is a long room. Stuffed into cases around the walls are the Lord's memorabilia that include strange looking bats of past cricketing greats and a few odd balls. It is unwise, however, to ask the provenance of many of the pictures from the Colman bequest; it could be embarrassing.

To all lovers of cricket, Lord's is unique. Not only is it the place where some of the finest cricket is to be seen, it is a meeting place of all lovers of the game. Even if it has rained for days, the pitch is sodden, the weather forecast promises more rain, electric storms and possibly hail (typical English cricketing weather), and the slimmest chance of play, hundreds of cricketophiles will converge from all corners of the country to that cathedral of cricket in the vain hope of watching a match and the certainty of meeting their friends.

On Test Match days, the pavilion is packed with members, mostly wearing their MCC ties that resemble strawberry jam on buttered toast – red and gold – although the *cognoscenti* tend to wear some other cricketing tie. You can watch from the Long Room (at least warm in cold weather and closest to the bar), or from one of the many terraces on the Pavilion or stands around the ground. Wherever you view from, conversation during play is the same:

a. silence;
b. a series of grunts.

Lengthy conversation during play:

a. 'good ball';
b. 'bad luck';
c. 'well played';
d. 'do wish they wouldn't hug and kiss on the field'.

One of the most prestigious invitations is to view a Test Match from the President's Box. As boxes go, it is disappointing, being modern and functional with exposed, grey-painted brickwork. The only splash of colour is provided by the yellow and red (MCC colours) plastic chairs. However, there is a splendid view of the wicket and other stands. The secretary's box in the Grand Stand is more traditional and in keeping with the place but still not exceptional. What sets the President's Box apart is the lavish lunch and tea, a healthy supply of drink and a smart guest list of twenty-four that will include:

a. your host, the President;
b. the President's wife – women are not allowed in the pavilion;
c. the High Commissioner of the country that is playing;
d. the chairman of the company sponsoring the Test Match;
e. any of the more ancient cricketing greats, like G. O. (Gubby) Allen, E. W. Swanton, the Bishop of Liverpool, Lord Home, P. B. H. May, Colin Cowdray, Doug Insole.

At least in that box, if you miss anything exciting, you can see the action replay on the television in the corner. If you are very brave and no one is looking, you can also turn over to watch the racing on the other channel. Such action, however, invariably invites a 'Bateman cartoon' response from your fellow guests.

The Eton and Harrow match at Lord's used to be a popular social occasion when it was held during Long Leave (summer half-term), not least for the boys as it meant an extra half day away from school. Then, there was a mêlée of morning coats and top hats, of chiffon dresses and straw boaters – those still at school wore *boutonnières* (Harrovians wore dark-blue cornflowers) and carried silver canes with either light or dark blue tassels. It was best to arrive by coach and four.

Today, it is held in July during the school holidays and, although the standard of cricket is still the same, the match is poorly attended. There is hardly a top hat to be seen and there is usually only one coach parked at the side of the ground. What is remembered (and often quoted in the House of Lords when debating football hooliganism) is the hostility between the rival groups. The last of many brawls and top hat bashing was in 1954 when Harrow won by nine wickets and the Eton boys stormed their changing-rooms.

Whatever the adversity, the English still manage to play and watch cricket. During the Boer War, the Boers took Sunday off for church and prayer, the British troops played cricket – at least until a few warning shots put them off. The English, after all, are not a religious race, but they did invent cricket, which gives them a sense of eternity. It is no coincidence that the weather vane over the score board at Lord's depicts Old Father Time at the wicket.

The All England Lawn Tennis and Croquet Club Championships at the end of June is the finest celebration of the game in the world. Despite the changing scene outside, Wimbledon remains a bastion of tradition. To the top professional tennis players, Wimbledon is still *the* tournament to win.

The English are masters at organizing such events discreetly yet with a great deal of panache, which makes it exciting for spectators and players alike. To gain admission to the hallowed Centre Court, you, like hundreds of thousands of other would-be spectators, can ballot for your tickets. Alternatively, you can pay a great deal of money (around £20,000) to be a debenture holder which will give you two 'free' tickets every day for the fortnight. Debentures come up every five years for sale through the Stock Exchange. If you are one of the four hundred members of the All England Club, then you are really privileged, with your own seats enjoying a good view of the Centre Court as well as the Royal Box. Unless you are invited as an ex-Wimbledon champion, or step over the closed waiting list of eight hundred hopefuls into dead men's shoes (one as unlikely as the other), it is better to be invited to join the Royal tennis groupies in the Royal Box. The advantages of such an invitation are:

a. you will be escorted to a cacophony of police sirens through the Wimbledon traffic to the front door (even called the Royal Steps) of the All England Club;
b. you do not have to sit in a traffic jam while the Royal party sail by in an aura of noisy blue light;
c. you will be the envy of thirty thousand in the Centre Court plus many millions watching on television;
d. you never know whom you might sit next to.

Once you arrive at the Royal Steps, you will be met by the Chairman, 'Buzzer' Haddingham M.C., and taken up the left-hand staircase to the pine-panelled Royal Sitting Room with the Royal Drinks Tray (note light green thick-pile Wilton carpet closely resembling astro-turf), the Royal Lavatories, the Royal Dining Room and the Royal Terrace, all of which are important for your enjoyment of the afternoon. Pre-prandial drinks follow, where

you meet the other forty guests lucky enough to be invited to the Royal Box. These might easily include:

    a. not the Queen, Prince Philip or Prince Charles, although the Queen is the Patron of the All England Club;

    b. any other member of the Royal Family especially:
       i. the Princess of Wales
      ii. the Duke and Duchess of Kent
     iii. the children, brothers and sister of the Duke and Duchess of Kent

iv. anyone related to the Princess of Wales or the Duke and
    Duchess of Kent, however far removed, such as ex-King
    Constantine of Greece or Jackie Stewart;
c. any relation or colleague of the Prime Minister, including
   high Anglicans;
d. the Ambassador or High Commissioner of any friendly country;
f. the Committee of the All England Club, who have their own
   side of the Box.

After a civilized luncheon in the Royal Dining Room you make
your way along a short landing to the Box, pausing, as Nanny
always said, 'to make yourself comfortable for the journey' in the
rather twee, highly interior decorated, Royal Lavatory. Glance at
the seating plan on the wall to your left as you enter the Box and
go to your appointed seat over the astro-turf that closely resembles
the Wilton carpet.

With luck, you will be in the front row and so amongst the
plethora of Kents, Spencers or the Cabinet Minister of the day,
not to mention those who really know what is happening on the
Centre Court. Apart from the obvious joys of sitting in the front
row, you are also locked into the results service of other matches
on a television monitor. If it is a little chilly, then you will be given
a light rug for your knees. During play, gasps, grunts and a light
clap will suffice, but inter-set conversation needs more thought:

a. to any of the Spencer sisters try
    i. the joys of young motherhood
    ii. what a pity that appendicitis robbed your mother of the
        chance to play at Wimbledon
    iii. how professional tennis beats polo as a spectator sport;
b. with the Duke and Duchess of Kent discuss:
    i. how professionals have altered Wimbledon since 1968 –
       colour your argument with 'If you can meet with Triumph
       and Disaster, And treat those two imposters just the
       same'
    ii. anything mechanical;
c. with any of the Committee of the All England Club discuss:
    i. how professionals have altered Wimbledon since 1968 –
       do not colour your argument with quotation from 'If' –

they will recognize it from the inscription over the door to the Centre Court

ii. the new meaning of the 'Tennis Court Oath', unless a French Monarchist is present

iii. anything to do with the Royal Air Force – the All England Club is a stronghold of the 'boys in blue'.

As Wimbledon is dominated by foreigners, you can feed a few professional terms and nick-names into your conversation:

a. waxed out – Anglo-American. Translation: he/she lost badly;
b. tanked the match – Anglo-American. Translation: he/she lost deliberately;
c. the Borg top spin – Anglo-Swedish. Translation: a seemingly impossible shot where the ball lies doggo on court;
d. the Borgette – Franco-American. Translation: Catharine Tanvier who can emulate Borg's top-spin;
e. the poet – Anglo-Argentine. Translation: Guillermo Vilas;
f. The Rabbit – Anglo-American. Translation: Wendy Turnbull.

Men should not remove their jackets before the HRH of the day (the *Duc du Jour*), nor depart for tea and/or strawberries and cream. When the first match is over, or before if it is not worth watching, you will leave for tea and/or a drink. While most drinking in the afternoon is generally frowned upon, especially in Royal Circles, Pimms is acceptable, which is strange, because it is highly alcoholic despite its infantile ingredients of fruit salad and lemonade. However, the tea is perfectly good (Indian and China) and there really is 'honey still for tea'.

After tea, you may or may not be allowed to watch another match but it is essential that you depart with your host as otherwise you will be stuck in the traffic jam of those still trying to arrive before the end of the day's play. Privileged yes, but the best way to view Wimbledon.

## THE HENLEY ROYAL REGATTA

If your advertising agency invites you to Henley, at all costs go. You will be splendidly fed and watered in their private tent on the Berkshire Bank; you may even glimpse an oarsman on the river. But this is not what Henley Royal Regatta is all about. The Royal Regatta is one of the very few sporting events in the world where no advertising is allowed, either on the banks or in the stands, either in the programme or on the boats, and certainly not on the oarsmen who compete solely for a cup, the Honour and the Glory. This is the spirit that has ruled Henley since 1839 and keeps it as the premier regatta in the world both for rowing and as a social occasion. Go to Nottingham or Lucerne and you will see some splendid rowing, but there will be nobody to lunch with. Henley is a truly British sporting event, rigidly administered by gentlemen for other gentlemen who are watched and applauded by yet more gentlemen and their attendant women. As with all truly British sporting events, it is as important to view it from the right place, in the right clothes, and with the right people, as to view it at all.

These vantage points are either:

a. the Stewards' Enclosure – for which you will need a voucher from a member or badges from a generous member, and do not bother to go if you do not have one. Once inside, make for the bandstand, where a good regiment will be playing martial music and selections from *My Fair Lady*. More important, it is within striking distance of:
   i. the champagne bar
   ii. the Pimms bar
   iii. the liqueurs bar
   iv. the loos
   v. the stands and deck chairs where you can actually watch a race;
b. the Senior Stewards' Enclosure – for which there are no vouchers, only personal invitations from senior stewards. Their sanctuary is guarded by gnarled and boatered doorkeepers who have memories like computers. The atmosphere here is hushed (most senior stewards are Very Old Rowing Men) but it does have the advantage of the Floating Stand, set at an angle to the finish, which is the best place to watch a close fought race and be introduced to the hierarchy.

If you are a rowing man you will have your kit (do not worry

if it does not fit – no one else's does). If not, a grey flannel
suit and box brogues are suitably self-effacing; an MCC or Eton
Ramblers tie will invite amused, but tolerant, incredulity. You will
find that the inhabitants of the Stewards' Enclosure are divided
into three categories:

a. Old Rowing Men – some are Very, Very Old Rowing Men but the plumage is unmistakable:
  i. blue boating jacket with appropriate buttons
  ii. very old and very faded rowing cap over very weather-beaten face – the smaller the peak, the older the cap and wearer
  iii. very distinguished tie
  iv. white duck trousers held up by second very distinguished tie
  v. pink socks;
b. Young Rowing Men – who will imperceptibly become Old Rowing men but are still rowing:
  i. school or college blazer, still rather new
  ii. straw boater over healthy but weather-beaten face
  iii. white duck trousers either hitched high to show off pink socks or worn rather low because the owners have not been elected to Leander yet;
c. women – wives, sisters, cousins, girl-friends or aunts. Whatever the weather they will be wearing silk or chiffon dresses and the fashionable hat; their credo female is that neither rain nor champagne spots.

All three categories will be intermittently watching the rowing and intermittently talking about it, and the rowing is intermittently why you are here on the banks of the Thames, on the green grass, under an English summer sky, watching an exacting sport once largely reserved for aspirants to Holy Orders or the Sudan Civil Service. Knowledgeable interest and discreet partisanship is well advised and almost as effective camouflage as a very distinguished tie.

Races to watch:

a. The Grand Challenge Cup – the oldest and grandest Henley cup. Cheer for Harvard or Leander. If anyone else wins, exclaim stuffily that they 'came on amazingly in training';
b. The Diamond Sculls – one of the most prestigious sculling races in the world, although nowadays the winner only collects silver sculls and miniatures at that. If an English entry should fail, mutter darkly about East German shamateurs;

c. The Ladies' Challenge Plate – which with truly English logic has nothing to do with ladies, who, until recently, were not allowed to compete in any Henley event. Furthermore, the plate is a cup. Being a race primarily for university colleges, and mostly Oxbridge ones at that, it provides pointers to an endless conversation about who might get a blue next year;

d. The Princess Elizabeth Cup, which really is a cup, for schools' eights. Each crew member hopes that a good performance here will make up for poor 'A' level grades. Comment on the difference a really enthusiastic headmaster makes.

All of which, if done with restrained brio (in the case of the Princess Elizabeth cup with as much noise as you like), will have put you on nodding terms with most of those around you. Concentrate on:

a. Peter Coni QC – President of Henley but still probably too busy to talk as thinking about the permutations of someone else's divorce;

b. John Garton – ex-president of Henley, doyen of British rowing;

c. Lord Cottesloe – attar of Old Rowing Man, thrice distilled, and if you mention rowing you may well receive a spot-on resumé of the events at Bisley;

d. Lord Camoys – rowing or banking, but Henley is not really the venue for discussions of equity participation. Leave that for a shooting weekend at Stonor up the road;

e. any Burnell, Tinné, Erskine-Crum, Gladstone or Mynors, all of whom are cousins, since rowing men have married each others' sisters for generations;

f. any distinguished Old Rowing Man with an unfamiliar tie and nasal intonation – almost certainly an American East Coast Oarsman. Do not mention the Kennedys – Henley banned Joe Senior as an artisan;

g. anyone you recognize, if only to check on their host;

h. anyone who will invite you to Leander Club, which includes all the above, all rightful inhabitants of the Senior Stewards' Enclosure and a great many from the Stewards' Enclosure.

Leander is the club where the pink ties, socks, caps and hippos come from and to which all oarsmen aspire, not an eight's length away from the Stewards' Enclosure. There, below the club house, which closely resembles an overgrown Edwardian cricket pavilion, you can sit on the grass with a glass of Pimms at the end of the day and hear how this crew was 'well coxed', and that crew chose 'unsuitable riggers', and whether Dan Topolski will really coach Oxford yet again next year. It is the cynosure of English rowing and of Henley Regatta, a clubbable Edwardian institution of charm and friendliness.

Do not ask about:

a. the Club's sewerage system;
b. the Club subscription.

However, do ask about the provenance of the Club's Tissot, 'Henley 1878'; no one will know but they will have strong opinions on the subject, the argument will go on for hours and you will be asked to dinner and delicately sounded about becoming an associate member.

## FISHING

To those inflicted with a passion for fishing, little matters outside their piscatorial world. To them, fishing is the truest of field sports, where it is the thrill that you are, or may be, *going* to catch a fish that counts, rather than the fact that you have:

a. had value for your money;
b. caught something to go with your chips, or an embryo *truite aux amandes*;
c. caught a trophy worth stuffing and mounting that will be the envy of your friends.

Fishermen, and the term embraces many excellent female anglers too, are a snobbish lot when it comes to the game-fishing they favour. To the purists among them, the brown trout, or brownie (as opposed to that American interloper, the rainbow trout), is the only quarry worth catching, and that with a dry fly on the classic chalk streams, with their see-through water, in the south of England. For the best trout-fishing in the world, go no further than the Middle Test as a member or guest of the Houghton Club at Stockbridge in Hampshire.

The beat to that ichtylogical zenith is long (virtually since birth – like poets, fishermen are born or created soon after) as you need not only the right tackle, clothes and infinite knowledge, but also the right connections.

Your tackle is easily bought at Hardy's of Alnwick, in Pall Mall or at Farlow's up the road, opposite the Athenaeum. Neither is impossibly expensive, you are hard pressed to spend more than £500 on all your equipment. A glance at the Royal warrants on the wall assures you that you are in the best of company, the Prince of Wales, the Queen Mother, *et al*, and it is comforting to recall that George V, having been advised to send Thomas Hardy congratulations on his seventieth birthday, sent his royal felicitations to the only Hardy he knew – his rod maker. Quite right too: whitebait before literature. Anyway, whether royal or mortal, allow an assistant to steer you towards:

a. an 8½ foot carbon fibre trout rod 'middle to tip action', easier to use and lighter than the now old-fashioned split cane rods;
b. a Hardy reel – a mere marquis will do;
c. some American tapered floating line;
d. tapered leader, 2–3 lb breaking strain;
e. a box of suitable flies. Resist the temptation to plump for those flies which look as if they belonged in an American's hat and those tied to seduce you rather than the fish.

Those who fish have their own favourite and/or lucky garb, none of which is remotely smart. Old school fishers have a well-cut jacket, aged and baggy – something reminiscent of a Conservative fête in Hampshire, Gloucestershire or Buckinghamshire (where Conservatives abound). Such jackets, like you as a proficient fisher of trout, will take approximately twenty years to mature. To complete the picture, equip yourself with a tie (invariably with a fish motif), and one pair each of polaroid glasses, scissors and chest-high waders (unlike the American's hat, they have no flies). Do not forget such necessary extras as a landing net and a creel.

There is no short-cut to experience, but if you keep at it, you will begin to understand:

a. what is going on inside that fishy little brain;

140

b. the myriad of fishing books starting with Piers of Fulham's work in the fourteenth century;

c. fishing language generously spiced with all too familiar terms from your private school – a flogger, a good beat, whipped to a white lather, a rod licence.

## *TROUT*

However proficient you are at catching trout, you still need the best contacts to be elected to the Houghton Club. With just twenty-two members it is the most exclusive fishing club in the world, a reputation it has enjoyed since its founding in 1822. It is every dry fly fisher's dream to fish the fifteen miles of riverbank on the Middle Test, either as a guest or, better by far, as a member. By tradition you do not apply for membership, but are invited to join after fishing as a guest and convincing everyone that you are not only a fisherman of surpassing skill but a convivial one as well.

Members are allowed to bring one guest each per day. Royal guests are not uncommon, with Lord Tryon and the Hon. Edward Adeane as members. The Drummonds do well with the Earl of Perth and his two sons, Lord Strathallan and the Hon. James all members. The Duke of Northumberland, like Hardy's also from Alnwick, is another in their riparian ranks. Lord Inchcape occasionally steams in. There is a good supply of surgeons, their concentration and deft fingers for tying flies are equally useful in their profession. The same is true of barristers who cast, catch, play and land both in court and on the river bank.

Entry to the Houghton Club is possible through a member resigning (rare) or by way of dead men's breast-high waders. Nonagenarians automatically become honorary members, which seems to increase their longevity. Since all fishermen believe the Babylonian proverb (later used on many occasions by the United States piscatorial President, Herbert Hoover) 'the gods do not deduct from man's alloted span the hours he spent in fishing', you are in for a long wait. Once you have been elected a member you pay:

a. entry fee £5000 – non returnable;

b. further debenture of £2000 – returnable to your heirs;

c. annual fee of £1200 – very reasonable by comparison with neighbouring chalk-streams.

Once you are elected, you can fish those exquisite, well-stocked waters with their manicured banks alongside your fellow members and their hopeful guests. You can also stay in the club's own hotel, the Grosvenor, in the middle of Stockbridge, and use the famous Houghton Club room with its bow window over the front door, stuffed fish and equally stuffed leather arm chairs and sofa. If you have stayed the night, you meet your fellow members over breakfast to the sound of rustling cornflakes and pages of *Salmon and Trout* (never the *Angling Times* – far too coarse). After breakfast, the senior member will ask where everyone would like to fish and then allocates the beats. There is, of course, plenty of room for members and their guests to fish, a fact that prompted one member to write:

> Of port and wine I've had my fill,
> I think I'll wander by the Mill,
> And if it's all the same to you,
> I think I'll fish Atwoods too.

You can fish right through the trout season – April until September. However, watch out for:

a. duffers' fortnight in early June – the time which is too much of a good thing for the trout, who gorge themselves on those tasty nymphs who become spinners (mayflies who drop their eggs on to the water before dropping dead themselves). Try offering them an imitation of another fly as a little light relief in their diet;

b. doing a Bengough – the eponym of the late member with a proclivity for falling in.

The most sensible thing to do is to stroll over the road to the stew-ponds and discuss the fishing prospects with the water bailiff, Mick Lunn. The Lunn family are now synonymous with

the Houghton Club, having been head bailiffs since 1886, a span of three generations. He might recommend a mayfly (if you tied [made] it yourself; do not make yourself the hero of the apocryphal story in which a natural mayfly paid the fisherman the compliment of mounting his fly in the air as he cast). A Lunn Particular is also a particularly good fly – when the inventor was introduced to a Hardy copy, the old man merely replied, 'Well, they got the hook right!'

Once on your beat, you can get down to the serious business of fishing in your own time, in your own way. Each beat is different, some better than others – the Doctor's Dipping Place is not so good now that the surgery drains no longer go straight into the water. Single out your fish for catching – nothing under a pound nor a grayling (the only other fish likely to take your fly).

You will never forget the experience: the warm summer day, the wide water meadows, the different greens of the river weed, the water voles and dragonflies on the river, the fall of the light and the ripple of the water. And as you stroll back to lunch you will remember how you placed your fly with a perfect cast upstream of the grey-brown shape rhythmically moving its gills; how the warm summer breeze and lazy current carried your beautifully tied fly downstream; how, in one fluid movement, that blunt snout took the fly with a 'pop' followed by a surge of boiling water and clouds of muddy silt, and how you played your monster fish, maybe all of a few ounces, and landed it on the bank to the grunt of your ghillie. It is the perfect way to spend April to September.

As the light fails, it is time to return to your room, a bath and the first of many drinks – help yourself and enter it in your own book. The Houghton is a club where members are expected to stay for dinner, even if they are local. Before dinner, the senior member present will enter in the journal all the fish caught that day, where and on what fly. Unless you draw like Landseer, a past member, do not be tempted to sketch on the hallowed pages. Dinner, a moderate menu that rarely includes trout, follows with much more to drink, then and after. The cellar varies with members – one American guest donated three thousand bottles of Jack Daniels, now long gone. However, in good clubable fashion, port is drunk in quantity. If you are really keen, the moon is full and the sedges are hatching, then you can go off after dinner to fish again.

When you finally go to that great chalk-stream in the sky, where the trout are so difficult that they can not be caught, hope that your fellow members of the Houghton Dry Fly Fishers Club will carve on your tombstone:

*Magnus Piscator Erat*


## SALMON

To the purist trout fisherman, salmon fishing is for the 'chuck and chance it' brigade. Salmon fishers refute such a slight; they believe that their chosen sport requires more knowledge, a more imaginative approach and better fishing techniques, in water that ranges in colour from the brown of the cheapest blended whisky to a torrent of thick, milk chocolate. However, there is no reason why you can not have the best of both waters and fish salmon as well as trout – at least the salmon is better eating and bigger, although this is of secondary importance (so they say).

The more you study the habits of salmon, or read the torrents of literature on *salmo salar*, the less you seem to understand your complex quarry. You will never know for sure why he will take the proffered tasty morsel of:

a. your fly, dressed like a tribal chief from darkest Africa;
b. a particularly smelly lure;
c. a silver spoon, someone else's birthright;
d. a worm – perish the thought but nonetheless effective, which is particularly interesting considering that salmon, when leaving the feeding grounds off the Faroes and Greenland, are on a fast until they return eight months later (assuming that they have escaped the Danish trawls, the estuary netters, poachers and other skilled fishers before you).

Killing salmon rests largely on your skill at:

a. interpreting the conditions and colours of the water and sky;
b. reading your thermometer and
c. listening to your ghillie – who will not be sparing with his advice.

Killing the best salmon in the best (i.e. the most difficult and testing) conditions depends largely on being able to fish on:

a. the Helmsdale – excellent fishing, very much a family river but now better known for gold than salmon to the chagrin of the six riparian owners like Sir Anthony Nutting, or the descendants of the great George McCorquodale. Beats operate on strict rotation, so are never overfished;
b. the Naver, Caithness – more good fishing up to pre-War standard. Best stretch owned by the Duke of Roxburgh (see below) who owns six lodges in his twenty-four miles. Only one man and a woman allowed per beat.

The major rivers are all good in their own way but suffer from the fact that they are large and thus more subject to the unsportsmanlike attentions of poachers, polluters and netters. Beware of complaining about the effect of Royal over-netting to the Queen, for you will be referred to the Government, who will pass you on to the Secretary of State for Scotland, who will refer you to the Queen. However, good sport is to be had on:

a. the Spey – home of the Spey cast (a short, natty little half-cast needed to overcome overhanging trees);
b. the Dee – best places on Balmoral beats a secret between the Prince of Wales and Fleet Street reporters and photographers (tabloid only);
c. the Tay – of William MacGonigal fame. Good autumn fish best caught on the Earl of Mansfield's banks;
d. the Tweed – good in parts – go for the Upper Floors beats as guest of the Duke of Roxburgh. It is better to be a guest as
   i. you do not have to pay £2000 plus for a week's fishing
   ii. you stay in Floors Castle
   iii. you do not have to stay in His Grace's hotel, Sunlaws in Kelso, with other fishing bores
   iv. you have the chance to catch a great autumn salmon (no nets downstream) – the record Tweed salmon stands with a Mr Pryor who caught a 57½ pounder in 1886.

For this legendary autumn run of salmon on the Tweed, usually between mid-October and mid-November, you will need:

a. a fourteen foot carbon fibre rod complete with reels and line and cast;
b. a box of flies that includes Mr Pryor's fly, a Silver Wilkinson, a Blue and/or Silver Doctor, a Garry Dog (named after the inventor's dog whose hair was the main component), a Durham Ranger, Thunder and Lightning (a real killer), a Jock Scott, the best known salmon fly – tie it yourself if you have ready access to the feathers of a golden pheasant, ostrich, toucan, Indian crow, turkey, peahen, florican, bustard, peacock, teal, mallard, gallina, jungle cock, blue chatterer, macaw, and swan (dyed of course); and a Toppy for good measure;
c. a good pair of waders and warm stockings (two pairs);
d. a wading stick or a boat depending how far out you wish to go;
e. a priest, not for absolution but a hefty stick for 'dealing' with your salmon;
f. a thermometer, for the river only, clearly marked at the magic figure of 48°F.

Kitted out and assigned to your beat – hope for the fast-running narrow neck of the Ferry Pool or the deep pools, Garden Wall or the Putt – watch out for the serious Tweed *salmo* gaffs of:

a. bringing a gaff within one mile of the sacred banks;
b. calling your boatman (a splendid breed of knowledgeable Border men) a ghillie;
c. bait-fishing or spinning after 15 September, or worse, any time with prawns, shrimps, plugs or worms;
d. fishing at all after 30 November;
e. fishing on a Sunday;
f. fishing for trout on a Sunday with a larger fly;
h. fishing the Duke of Roxburgh's own beat on a Saturday;
i. forgetting to tip the ghi . . . er . . . boatman – £5 per day, £30 for the week;
j. forgetting to thank His Grace (on penalty of getting no repeat invitation).

Thus armed, you are ready to start fishing. If fishing from a boat, your boatman will take you to the right places and generally look after you. He will also be on hand when you catch your salmon (plural) and be ready with advice and net for landing same. Whatever you hear on and off the bank, no one can match William Scrope (author of *Days and Nights of Salmon Fishing* 1843) when he wrote, 'Your fly, or its exact position, should never be lost sight of; and you should imagine every moment of the livelong day that an extraordinary large salmon is coming at it.'

## YACHTING

There are older yacht clubs in the world – for instance the Royal Cork Yacht Club, founded in 1720; there are some with infinitely higher subscriptions, the New York Yacht Club for one; but there is none more exclusive nor more difficult to join than the Royal Yacht Squadron. 'The Squadron', as it is imperiously known, is at home in a sixteenth century castle softened into grand domesticity that commands the harbour of Cowes on the Isle of Wight – 'the most impregnable fortress ever held by the aristocracy of England against the storms and sieges of the combined forces of the rich merchants and the bourgeoisie.' It is the bastion of all that is exclusive in the sailing world, although membership is not necessarily the goal of all who take sailing, in particular, racing, seriously (or so they say).

As with Field Marshals, membership is established at a set number – Field Marshals 12, RYS400 (700 if you include Naval members and Lams – lady associate members). Up to a few years ago, the Squadron had a reputation for consisting of wall-to-wall old buffers in blue blazers (with the right buttons), with gnarled hands that fitted exactly round a Gordon's gin bottle. Today, the membership is younger and dedicated to both sailing and racing. To join their gilded ranks, you must first solicit the aid of as many voting members as possible – do not waste your time on Naval members: they, like most Scottish and Irish peers, are non-voting and only pay, like the late Admiral of the Fleet Earl Mountbatten of Burma, the reduced one third subscription. Although the old salts on the committee used to be free with their blackballs (a certain grocer's ballot box resembled a pot of caviar, an industrialist's a field of rabbit-droppings), nowadays your entry does not go forward if the black balls are likely to fall. The annual dinner is held after the April elections and before Cowes Week in August, so that last ditch opponents to your entry do not have a chance to whip up support for their campaign against you. However, do not under any circumstances anticipate your election by pre-arranging a celebratory dinner at the Savoy for twenty-three of your closest friends. You will be elected because you are:

a. a good yachtsman – you may also happen to be an exiled king, but this on its own is not quite enough;
b. a good chap of the right vintage;
c. able to pay the entry fee and the annual subscription – the amounts are instantly forgotten as paid by banker's order.

Once you have been voted a member you will be entitled to the Squadron's privileges. You can:

a. use the place as much as you like. The Squadron is like a smart London club with the decor of a country house. The ladies' sitting room is slightly more chintzy than the main drawing room and library. Usually there is no bar, and a uniformed steward will bring your chosen drinks to the table at the press of a bell. Members' wives/girl-friends also do well with a luxurious bathroom complete with hairdryers and ironing boards. Note the original cartoons by Fluk in the members' changing room;
b. use the Squadron Trotts – a line of posts up-river where yachts are moored side by side;
c. enjoy the unrestricted use of the RYS launch – Andrew the boatman will take you from the Squadron Steps to your, or anybody else's boat, like HMY *Britannia*;
d. like HM the Queen on HMY *Britannia*, fly the White Ensign on your yacht if it is over ten tons;
e. wear the mess-kit – known as a bum-freezer. Messrs Gieves and Hawkes would be delighted to make up the short jacket, vest and trousers for you in dark blue barathea, complete with Squadron buttons, for around £500. Providing you do not change shape, it should last you all your life. Most members fancy themselves hugely in their mess-kit and wear it on every possible occasion. So that your wife/girl-friend is

not jealous, you can buy her a diamond and ruby RYS burgee from Garrards for £800 (more expensive on Cowes) which should also last her all her life.

As at your private school, you will be given a number but, unlike your school number, you move up as the older members move out (unless you are the Duke of Edinburgh who came in at number one). As with tradesmen, women are admitted into the castle so long as they use their own entrance (it is not that long since they were housed in a harem within the grounds and only allowed in on special nights such as the Squadron Ball). On quiet nights, women can steal out of their sitting room in the west wing and slip into the library, although permission must first be obtained from the senior member in the room (look him up in the register outside).

The more serious 'yachties' of the Royal Ocean Racing Club or the Royal Thames Yacht Club (among many others) regard the Squadron, with their self-perpetuating eliteness and traditions, as something of a joke (although this does not stop them trying to gate-crash their parties). With a few notable exceptions, the active Squadron members are mostly day-sailors with fast racing-yachts such as Dragons, X-boats and Darings, an exciting thirty-seven foot long boat local to Cowes and raced by the gentry. The tradition of great racing yachts which ruled before the Second World War, with their tradesmen or industrialist non-Squadron owners, is still alive today. Although their boats are smaller, the money required to build them and the numbers of crew to race them remain roughly the same. The premier racing yachts are the 'Admiral's Cuppers' – any one of the five classes of Ocean Racers from which the Admiral's Cup team will be chosen.

You will be asked to race in one of these sophisticated and expensive machines if you are:

a. a 'gorilla' (a very strong amateur crew);
b. a computer boffin – since 1982, computers are allowed to process the data of wind, sea and sails to assist the navigator;
c. a red-hot skipper (amateur, of course) the most enviable position of all - having the fun of racing without
   i. paying
   ii. being over-physical with sails

iii. being sick below over a computer;
d. the owner of the boat and paying for it all.

If you plump for the last option, you can, of course, combine any of the above roles – Graham Walker (last captain of the British Admiral's Cup Team) is an owner/gorilla on his boat *Indulgence* and takes his orders like a man from the skipper, Eddie Ward-Owen. A more satisfactory combination is owner/skipper, like Brian Saffery-Cooper who drives his own boat, *Whirlwind*, or Robin Aisher, who only gives up the wheel of his yacht, *Yeoman XXV*, to that Royal old sea dog, Baron Greenwich.

As an owner you will discover, all too quickly, that the two old clichés are true: a boat is a hole in the water through which you pour money, and sailing is standing under an ice-cold shower while your best friend tears up £5 notes, only now it is £50 notes. (Gordon Bennett's famous reply to the man who asked him if he was rich enough to own a yacht, 'if you have to ask yourself that question, you are definitely not rich enough', is as true today as it was in the 1920s.)

Regardless of the type of sailing and racing you choose, the high point of the Needle for the yachting fraternity (and sorority) is Cowes Week held during the first week of August. It is organized by a powerful body known as the Cowes Combined Clubs, and is attended by all those who are remotely distinguished in the yachting world and by those who would like to be thought of in such terms, but in fact go for the parties.

For that one week that little island, about the size of Grenada, is invaded and becomes a seething mass of boat and humanity as:

a. there is not much room to sail. The number of boats of different classes, the double tides, the wash from the Townsend Thoresen ferries, the enormous tankers and cruise ships, make racing that much more interesting and thus satisfy the British love of a challenge;
b. there is not much room for your boat, unless you are fortunate enough to be on the Squadron Trotts. There are only two marinas, so that yachts are moored six to eight deep and only the public courtesy of the English prevents Cowes rivalling Los Angeles in the murder league tables;

*152*

c. there is not much room for people – as a member of the Squadron, you can ballot for a room for Cowes Week on the Glorious First of June, but if you are a new member it is diplomatic not to apply. Favoured invitations come from:

   i. Sir Max Aitken – his extremely comfortable converted sail-loft, *Prospect*, is the heart of the social side of Cowes Week. Staying with him has the added advantage that it is your passport to every party. If you are not actually racing, you can watch some of it from the balcony or be taken out in your host's vast 'gin palace', *Blue Max*

   ii. Basil Reginald Vincent-Ziani de Ferranti (known as Boz from his initials rather than any Dickensian forebear) and his wife, Hilary – genial hosts with a comfortable house, *Providence*. As both own and race Darings, his *Ding Dong*, hers *Finesse*, your fellow guests tend to be other Daring owners. A major advantage of staying here is warming up after a day's racing in the sauna bath

   iii. The Duke of Edinburgh – to stay aboard HMY *Britannia*. This is also comfortable and amusing, with the younger and sailing members of the Royal Family such as Princess Alexandra

   iv. The Trinity House tender – this is more practical than comfortable but it does afford a splendid view of the proceedings.

To those who take Cowes Week seriously, social and sailing, it is a punishing test of stamina, and only the fittest can survive the course. If you are not participating, like most who grace Cowes that week, you can enjoy watching the racing from the Squadron Lawn, now covered with a large marquee, and go to the endless drinks parties and balls. The best, naturally, is the most exclusive, naturally, and that is, naturally, the Squadron Ball, held first, naturally. Other balls, like the Royal Corinthian Yacht Club, the Royal London Yacht Club, the Island Sailing Club (be very polite to the security guards here, they all appear to be wardens from Parkhurst and Albany prisons) are also fun, as are most of the better drinks parties like those on Prospect, the Royal Naval Guardship or the Royal Yacht. The climax of the Week is the fireworks on Friday night which are best viewed from the Squadron Lawn or the terrace of Providence. Saturday night is the night of the Bembridge Ball where Bembridge matrons adjudge themselves superior to the Squadron reliving old rivalries of East Cowes versus West Cowes. You will certainly enjoy it, particularly if you have been there every summer for a bucket and spade holiday as a child. However, if you are in the Fastnet Race, you will have left that morning.

The Fastnet, 605 miles round the Fastnet Rock (off Cape Clear in Ireland) from the Squadron (where else?) and ending up with a party (what else?) at the Royal Western Yacht Club at Plymouth, is held every other year. If the tides are right, bang on nine o'clock the cannon on the terrace of the Royal Yacht Squadron sets off the Admiral's Cup contenders, from fourteen other countries (including Japan and Papua New Guinea) along with a sea of over 250 boats in a dozen other classes behind.

Through the years, it has become a deadly serious race. Long gone are the days when you could see, as in 1926, a female crew in plus-fours, galoshes and blue motor veils clutching golfing umbrellas, or, as recently as 1956, Baron de Rothschild and friends sitting down in black tie to dine aboard the Baron's yacht, served by four stewards. Today, comfort and a leisurely sail have been replaced by discomfort and damned hard work for all.

In your life on the micro-wave, you will:

a. eat all your meals, reminiscent of a Chinese take-away in their foil containers, on your lap – in bad weather all too literally;
b. use water sparingly, certainly not for drinking, as it is limited so as to improve your weight/power ratio to allow for the myriad of batteries required by the space-age instruments the navigator and computer-man demand;
c. become used to drinking your two beers (small) straight from the can that is covered with the flavour of your bilges;
d. collapse into your pipe cot (at best), a string hammock (at second best), the damp sails that line the cabin floor (at worst). After climbing exhausted into or on to whatever option is open to you, you will be immediately woken and shifted to the windward side. To add to the discomfort in foul weather, sails, which started the race as tightly packed

cubes, will gradually invade the saloon, wet, clammy and unfoldable;

e. invariably be in the watch that has a minimum of ten complete sail changes in the night.

There are years when the weather is warm and the sea friendly, when you spend most of the time with your legs over the windward side reading an improving book, but the Fastnet Race has more of a reputation as a 'tough bash to windward'. Sometimes, as in 1979, it is more than that: 'Some waves had boiling foam all over them, deep green from the disturbance of the water. Otherwise, the sea was black.' Weather like that is not only uncomfortable but also very frightening.

By the time you arrive in Plymouth at the end of the race, you will find that there is just enough time to make it to Scotland or Yorkshire for the start of the grouse season. Before you leave, there is a slim chance that you will be elected to a most exclusive club called 'The Imperial Poona Yacht Club'. It has no club house, just twenty-two members, and the Duke of Edinburgh as its president. At the annual meeting, a dinner, you will be given and called by an Indian name (like Umwallah). The members dine together and reminisce over the joys of sailing and racing, past, present and future.

# IN CELEBRATION OF
# THE BEST OF BRITISH

Your cot was made of Wycombe beech,
Your robe of Ulster lawn,
And if you learned to love your Nan
Far more than Muv, or Tom or Fan,
It was because she soon assessed
That you were British, quite the best.

Golden days on Bembridge sand,
Back to bed with bear;
Picking all those pheasants up;
Competing for a Pony Cup;
All these activities will hone
Your British face, your British bone.

Floreat – well, where you went,
Cranborne Chase or Eton;
And what you learned from Caesar's Gaul
Or 'Further Footsteps with St Paul'
Can only go to validate
That Best of British cannot date.

From Locks to Lobb's – not twenty yards
And just beyond is White's,
How strange that in this single street
Should rest your head, your friends, your feet.
But surely you are truly blessed,
Who knows that British is the best.

Huntsman builds you all your tweeds,
The pebbles come from Home,
And when you stalk on Kinlochewe
The German guests can freely view
A gentleman correctly dressed –
The British tailor'd at their best.

'They' say it's style that makes the man;
It could be argued so,
As, when the Briggs umbrella drops,
The single rain-washed taxi stops,
To demonstrate to all the rest
How the British do it best.

And if the City calls you now
To trade in stocks and shares,
The Bank gives you a yellow card
With smiles last seen in Weston's Yard,
And others in the One Square Mile,
Will also note the 'Lady's' smile.

That welcomes to our British shore
The Barings and their Bank,
So Seligman and Montagu
Rothschilds and the Goldschmids too
Can join the Hambros and attest
That British banking is the best.

Yet you don't wish to lay your head
Forever in the Met
A family should have some land,
Whose soil has passed from hand to hand
Of countless sons who passed the test
The Sporting Life, forever best.

Nor would you wish to bring your wife
To some small Chelsea flat.
For she was brought up to adore
Her children, horse-box, labrador,

And by an inbred instinct know
Just who's with whom at County Show.

So it's: 'Jamie, where's the meet today?'
'Poor Bounder's very lame'
And 'You have really promised Prue
That whatsoever else you do
The Volvo will be used to get
The stable-girl, and then the vet.'

But Thursday now, I tell you what,
The City's all agog
And Casenoves will only take
An hour to tell you what you'll make:
They've something in Japan – we'll meet
At one o'clock, by Jermyn Street.

Now have another Kummel, do!
It's years since lunch at Green's,
And Mathew Farrel thinks he'll see
Some hope for Charles and CTT
So you can dine, without a care
At Annabels in Berkley Square.

Dust to dust, the wheel it turns,
And that's the bloody point.
Your vault may just contain a bone,
Your name may weather on a stone,
But on your land your sons pursue
All that's right and entail'd too,
A yard of hunters, vintage port,
A pheasant wood, a tennis court,
To complement your lawyers' plan
And prove to all who makyth man,
That such a life you lived with zest
Was Very British, so the Best.